spin to knit

The Knitter's
Guide to
Making Yarn

Shannon Okey

INTERWEAVE PRESS
www.interweave.com

Photography: Joe Coca unless otherwise noted
Process photography: Christine Okey
Featured spinner photography: Shannon Okey

 Interweave Press LLC
201 East Fourth Street
Loveland, Colorado 80537 USA
www.interweave.com

Printed in China by C & C Offset Printing Co., Ltd.

Library of Congress Cataloging-in-Publication Data

Okey, Shannon, 1975
 Spin to knit : the knitter's guide to making yarn / Shannon Okey, author.
     p. cm.
 Includes bibliographical references and index.
 ISBN 10: 1-59668-007-5 (pbk.)
 ISBN 13: 978-1-59668-007-4 (pbk.)
 1. Knitting--Patterns. 2. Spinning. 3. Yarn. I. Title.
 TT820.O365 2006
 746.1'2--dc22

                                   2006005287

10 9 8 7 6 5 4 3 2

Acknowledgments

Without the love, help, and support of Tamas Jakab, I wouldn't be where I am right now. The same goes for our dachshund Anezka and naughty kitten Spike, to whom "help" means "drag all of Mommy's yarn from the studio into the dining room." Thanks to the three of you for loving me despite all the late dinners and missed walks while this was being written.

Thanks to Betsy Armstrong, Rebecca Campbell, and everyone at Interweave Press. The writing and editing process is made much more enjoyable by your clear love of what you do. Special thanks to Linda Ligon, for taking the time to talk with me about this book, and for suggesting someone write it in the first place, to Ann Budd for her thoughtful editing, and particularly to Lori Gayle for not only enduring the first draft of my patterns, but for making them even better with her input.

Thanks to my fairy knitmother Jillian Moreno, to Heather Brack, my sounding board, and to Amy Singer, who published my first article about spinning on Knitty.com. Special thanks to eagle-eyed Kristi Porter for her usual thoughtful editing and proofreading. Thanks to all my knitting friends online—some appear in this book, whether as featured spinners, yarn creators, or pattern contributors. Caroline Horner, Sue Jalowiec, Susan Ensor, and Heather Brack all pinch-knitted for me when time was tight (they'll never know how much they helped).

Thanks to Lynne Vogel, her workshop assistants Sandy Sitzman and Lori Lawson, and her students at the Shakerag workshops in Sewanee, Tennessee, for welcoming me and my camera into their classroom. Lynne's *The Twisted Sisters Sock Workbook* gave me the inspiration to experiment and play with dyes, following in the path of my knitting/spinning teacher ("guru"? the word would not be misused) Lucy Lee. I'm fortunate to know them both.

Thanks to Elizabeth Ashford and Cindy Howard-Gibbon at Foxglove Fiber Arts, Ashford's U.S. distributor, for providing supplies, particularly the portable Joy wheel I used when I was on the road for a month taking the featured spinner photos. (I could never imagine dragging my Elizabeth II wheel, nicknamed Queen Liz, in a suitcase. The Joy was, well, a joy.) Candi Cane, Kayt de Fever, Kim Werker, Jenny Koenig, and Rae Nester took turns feeding, housing, amusing and helping me that month, too. Thank you, friends.

And finally, big thanks to all the featured spinners and to the other talented spinners who provided yarn for the projects—I'm not sure who had more fun with your yarns, you or me!

Contents

Introduction

When you first learned to knit, someone probably told you that knitting is easy. After all, you only have to learn two things: knit and purl. It was a little more complicated than that, right? Both knitting and spinning are very simple at their most basic level, yet they allow for infinite variation, personalization, and a lifetime of learning possibilities. However, I can still confidently say that spinning is comprised of only two things: draft and twist. I'll even wager you can make yarn in less than five minutes.

Would you like to take me up on that bet?

Get a cotton ball from your bathroom cabinet and gently pull it into the longest strand you can manage without breaking it into pieces (you are "drafting" the fiber here). Put one end of the strand on your thigh. Roll the fiber with your other hand, picking it up and bringing it back to the starting point when you can't roll any farther. When you've got a good amount of twist built up, pick up the center of the strand with one hand and the two loose ends with your other. Allow the strands to twist together. Voilà—you've just spun your own yarn! Wasn't that easier than your first tortured row of stitches?

Why spin? There are so many commercial yarns available, after all—why waste valuable knitting time to make your own yarn? It's about control and creativity. It's also cost-effective once you have the basic equipment. You can make one-of-a-kind designer yarns for a fraction of the retail price. Their colors, style, and intended end use are all up to you . . . the possibilities truly are endless.

In this book, I'll not only show you how to spin yarn using your method of choice (spindle or wheel), but I'll also show you how to make the most of the yarn you spin. Many of the patterns combine commercial (or "millspun") yarn with handspun. You won't need to spin miles and miles of yarn before you can see knitted results.

Choosing the right pattern does make a difference. When I first learned to spin, I did it the hard way. I started with a raw fleece from a chocolaty-gray Maine ram named Eddie who had the temperament of a large, cuddly dog. I decided to knit a sweater, and I did absolutely everything "wrong," at least according to the conventional wisdom. (Sin #1 of many: starting to knit before I'd spun enough for the entire project.)

The sweater came out not only wearable, but beautiful. I remain convinced that it worked only because I chose an appropriate pattern that adapted well to the irregular yarn. (Beginner's luck may have played a part, too.) The sized patterns in this book will also adapt to your required measurements, no matter what kind of yarn you spin.

You don't need expensive equipment—in fact, it's possible to start with less than $20 in materials. Make a spindle from a CD, use your elbow for a niddy-noddy, buy a few ounces of fiber, and you're in business. Where you go from there is up to you.

My very first handspun yarn became the Eddie Sweater.

Equipment Overview

You need more than just needles to knit, and like any craft, there is a fine line between "useful tool" and "gadget purchased that collects dust." Spinning uses many of the same tools as knitting, as well as a few you may not have seen before.

Swift and Ball Winder

If you've managed to survive without a swift and a ball winder until now, you might want to acquire them before you spin too much yarn. A skein of yarn is placed on a collapsible swift, then the swift rotates as the ball winder is used to wind the yarn into a tidy center-pull ball.

A yarn swift holds a skein of yarn as it is wound into a center-pull ball on a ball winder.

WPI Gauge

WPI gauges measure the "wraps per inch" of a given yarn. You can use a pencil, a ruler, or a commercial WPI gauge—the result will be the same. Although it sometimes seems there will never truly be a standardized yarn system (see pages 57 and 126), WPI can be used to communicate consistent, measurable information about a yarn's actual weight, regardless of name. One person's worsted may be another's Aran weight!

To measure wraps per inch, take your tool of choice and roll a few inches of yarn around it. Grasp the yarn end against your tool and roll the tool to wind on the yarn. If you choose to wrap the yarn instead, don't wind too tightly. You'll distort the measurement by stretching the yarn. Each strand of yarn should just touch its neighbor. The number of strands in one inch is your WPI measurement. If your yarn is thick/thin or otherwise variable, wrap several inches and divide accordingly for accuracy.

WPI gauges are used to measure wraps per inch of yarn.

Niddy-noddy

The niddy-noddy, often called a "niddy" for short, is essential for winding skeins of yarn straight from the bobbin or spindle. It also comes in handy for other less conventional uses, like taking out overtwist in a yarn. Its name comes from a traditional rhyme sung while winding off the yarn: "Niddy noddy, niddy noddy, two heads, one body." Simply hold the center section and rotate your wrist as you wind the yarn around the two "heads."

Many niddys are collapsible (the "head" ends come off for storage), but don't be tempted to glue them in place! Storing your niddy flat with the heads pointed in the same direction is a space saver. You can also use the "body" piece as an impromptu nøstepinne to wind center-pull balls of yarn (see page 9).

Niddys come in different sizes. If you're unsure how long your niddy's skeins are, measure one complete wrap around the niddy. To determine the amount of yarn currently wound, count the strands in one section and multiply by the length of one wrap.

If all else fails, you've always got a niddy with you: your elbow. It's trickier to leave the singles there overnight, though.

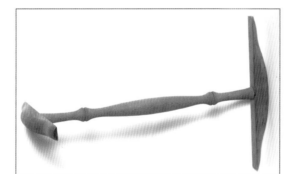

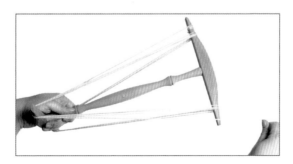

Use a niddy-noddy to wind your handspun into a tidy skein.

Yarn Meter

If you want to measure the yardage of your singles yarn as it moves straight from the bobbin or spindle to a ball winder, or if you have a lot to measure at once, use a yarn meter. You pass the yarn through the meter, which measures as the yarn moves. It doesn't measure heavy or lumpy yarns very well, which is a disadvantage for beginning spinners, but if you spin very fine yarn, it may come in handy for you.

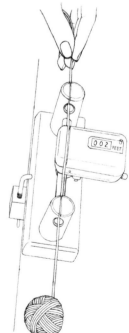

A yarn meter measures the yardage in a ball of yarn.

McMorran Balance

McMorran balances tell how many yards are in a given quantity of yarn based on a measurement of yards per pound. A metric version is also available.

Place a length of the yarn in question over the balance's arm and trim off yarn until the arm is once again level. Measure the resulting piece of yarn and multiply it by 100 to obtain the number of yards per pound. Weigh the yarn and calculate accordingly. It also comes in handy if you're spinning a large quantity of yarn (say, for a sweater) and want to do "quality control" between bobbins. It will work with heavier yarns, unlike a yarn meter.

A McMorran balance will help you determine how many yards are in a given quantity of yarn.

A Case for Nøstepinne

A nøstepinne (also nøstepinde or nystepinne, depending on whether you're Swedish, Danish, or Norwegian) is used to wind a center-pull ball of yarn. It can be anything from a elaborate, turned wood piece to the end of a spindle or wooden spoon. You can use the body of your niddy if at least one of the heads comes off.

Why use nøstepinnes when there are ball winders and swifts? They're portable, cheap, and if you spin very bulky yarn, or yarn with "additions" (such as the daisy yarn used in the May Day Hat, page 85), they might be your only option for making a center-pull ball. Here's how:

Grasping the nøstepinne in your nondominant hand, wrap several inches of yarn loosely onto the center. If you have an actual nøstepinne with a notch in the end, be sure to place the yarn end there so you can pull it out of the center when you're finished. If you're improvising, leave a length of yarn dangling by starting your wraps several inches into the yarn, or cheat by taping the end of the yarn to the nøstepinne's end before starting. The amount you wrap in the beginning will determine the height of the finished ball. You want it to be tight enough not to fall off as you wind, but loose enough to slide the ball off when you're finished.

When you've wound on the initial height of your ball, begin to wrap the yarn diagonally from the bottom right to the top left of the section (or vice versa), turning the nøstepinne as you do. Each diagonal wrap should snuggle next to the previous one, without overlapping. When you come to the first wraps, continue to wind right over them, and when you finish, gently slide the ball off the nøstepinne.

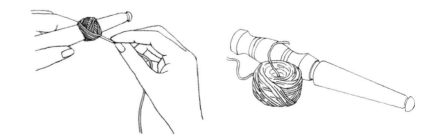

To create a center-pull ball, rotate the nøstepinne as you wrap the yarn diagonally from bottom right to top left.

Chapter 1

Fiber 101 for Knitters

Until now, you could rely on the label to tell you everything you needed to know about a particular yarn. Not if you make your own yarn! Here we'll discuss what you should know about commonly available spinning fibers, including appropriate uses and the formats in which they're sold. For example, while you probably wouldn't want to use alpaca in a felting project, you could spin and knit it into something that you'll want to wear close to your skin, such as a scarf.

SPINNING FIBER TYPES:
- Wool: various sheep breeds
- Camelids: alpaca, llama
- Angora: rabbit
- Mohair: goats
- Plant fibers: cotton, soy silk, bamboo
- Unusual spinning fibers: dog fur, buffalo, recycled fabric, and others

---

When you first learned to knit, you may have been told to start with pure wool yarn—it's flexible and forgiving of beginner mistakes. The same goes for spinning; learn with wool before moving on to plant or man-made fibers.

If you're allergic to wool, I recommend starting with silk or a silk/lyocell blend. You might also try merino wool, which isn't as irritating for some people. If you have a choice, select a fiber with the longest possible staple length (see page 12).

In order to compare/contrast the characteristics of spinning fibers, the following terms and definitions come in handy. Some apply to all fiber types, some only to one or two.

Bradford count/micron count: These numeric measurements indicate the fiber's fineness. In the Bradford system, the higher the number, the finer the fiber. It corresponds to the number of 560-yard skeins that can be spun from one pound of wool. Merino, one of the finest wools, can be as high as an 80 Bradford count. Corriedale, an average wool, usually measures around 60. Micron count, on the other hand, is based on the actual average diameter of a single fiber, so lower numbers equal finer fiber.

"[Breed name] cross": The fiber in question is not from a purebred animal. If there's only one name before "cross," chances are it is very similar to the breed in question.

Crimp: Crimp, or the degree of inherent waviness in the fiber, varies widely depending on the fiber and the animal breed. Fiber with a high degree of crimp tends to be finer and easier to spin, because each strand "sticks" better to its neighbors.

Locks: Some goats and sheep breeds have coats that are separated into distinctive curly locks. Kid (baby) mohair and Lincoln sheep are two examples of this. Locks can be carded like any other fiber, spun directly, or spun whole into other yarns for special effects.

Resilience/elasticity: If you hold a sample of a given fiber between your two hands and stretch it; the amount of stretch and how quickly it bounces back to the original length indicate resilience and elasticity. Wool has a high degree of inherent resilience; camelid fibers do not. This is why sweaters of pure alpaca have a tendency to "grow" over time. The same sweater knitted from wool would bounce right back to its original shape and size after washing and blocking.

Staple length: This is the average length of the individual fibers in a given sample of the fiber. Individual sheep breeds, and other fiber animals or plants have fairly predictable staple lengths. Staple lengths affect the way in which a particular fiber can be processed and spun.

Superwash: Superwash wool is treated to resist shrinking and felting, much like superwash yarns. The process alters the fiber's structure slightly, which causes it to take up dye faster and feel slightly different to the touch than untreated wool.

Undercoat: Some types of sheep, Cashmere goats, dogs, bison, and other fiber animals have two coats. The outer coat consists of "guard hairs," which are wirelike and stiff. The undercoat is soft and fluffy; removing the guard hairs is necessary to spin a high-quality yarn. This labor-intensive process is what makes cashmere so expensive.

Fiber Breed Characteristics

The characteristics of a given fiber or breed will help you make an appropriate choice for the yarn you want to spin. Soft, fine, crimpy merino wool is perfect for scarves, turtlenecks, and anything you'll wear close to the skin. Churro sheep produce tough-wearing fiber that withstands hard use in the Navajo rugs woven from it. Blending alpaca 50/50 with even the most generic wool will give the yarn (and items knitted from it) more "memory," or the ability to spring back into shape. Cotton is durable, but doesn't have much bounce, which makes it tough for some beginning spinners (not to mention its staple length is very short).

Some of the most common sheep breeds you'll encounter as a handspinner are Corriedale, Romney, Border Leicester/Blue-Faced Leicester, Cormo, Targhee, Shetland, Wensleydale, Jacob, Coopworth, Merino, and "Colonial." Note that "Colonial" is not a single breed, but a blend of various similar wool fibers, often similar in feel to Corriedale. Consider it generic, medium-staple length wool for the purpose of making comparisons.

Corriedale and Romney wools are my personal recommendations for beginning spinners. The fiber format you choose makes a difference, too. Not everyone wants to start with a raw fleece, though I will describe how to dive right in if someone drops a garbage bag of straight-from-the-sheep fuzz on your doorstep.

Fiber Formats

Once you've settled on a fiber, you need to choose a format. Fibers come in all shapes and sizes and are prepared in many different ways. Carded fiber types include sliver (long continuous strands of carded wool, usually packaged in large rolls that are ready for spinning), batts (thick rectangles that look like quilt fiberfill, mostly used for felting, but can also be divided and spun), roving (similar to sliver, but with a small amount of twist), and pencil roving (very thin roving). The fibers in a carded preparation are mostly aligned, but they can also cross over and around each other.

Combed wool that looks like roving is called top, and the two words are often used interchangeably. Top is considerably denser than roving and needs to be predrafted before use (see page 30). Many commercial handspinning fibers labeled "roving" are actually top. The fibers are aligned all in one direction, and the surface will feel very smooth if you run it through your hand.

Top tends to be easier for new spinners because it's so easy to manipulate and is readily available. But if you're trying to answer the eternal question "What on earth do I do with this plastic bag of fuzz someone just dumped on me?" you'll need to know how to prepare your own fiber, too. Mention you're learning to spin and garbage bags full of fiber magically appear from out of nowhere, especially if you live in a suburban or rural area. I'm not kidding—try it! It's like letting your own personal spinning genie out of the bottle.

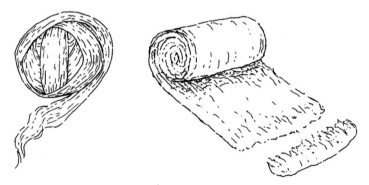

Most carded fiber comes in sliver (left) and batts (right).

Sheep to Shawl: Or "What Do I Do with This Bag of Fleece?"

The instructions here apply mostly to wool; if you're lucky enough to receive an alpaca or llama fleece as a gift, you may want to wait until you have a little more experience under your belt. These fleeces contain no natural lanolin like wool, and don't usually need to be cleaned as aggressively. They're also more challenging to spin in their unprocessed state.

Although some spinners prefer to spin "in the grease" (without cleaning the wool first), it's a good idea to give your first fleece at least one good washing. Start by inspecting it closely: spread out a clean sheet and unroll the fleece. If it's been "well-skirted," the seller will have removed the dirtiest, most matted parts around the hindquarters and tail. If not, pull them off now.

If you see bits of hay or leaves, pick the larger ones out. Some sheep wear canvas coats when

Wash fleece before spinning to prevent damaging your spinning equipment.

they're out in the field to keep "VM" (vegetable matter) out of the fleece. If your fleece doesn't have very many of these bits, chances are it's good quality. "Low VM" is used as a selling point with raw fleeces.

Fill your bathtub with the hottest water you can. Wool is very similar to our hair in structure, so I use cheap shampoo designed for oily hair to clean it. Mix in the shampoo after the bathtub has filled to prevent excess suds. Next, deposit part of the fleece on top of the water (depending on how much you have, you may need to divide the fleece into thirds to fit it into your bathtub without layering). Using a long-handled wooden spoon or other utensil, push the fleece gently under the water. Resist the temptation to stir—you don't want to tangle or felt it. Allow the fleece to soak; the water will likely turn a yellow-brown immediately. When the water begins to cool down to room temperature, drain the tub. Hold the fleece back gently with your spoon to keep it from going down the drain. You can now skip ahead and spin the excess water out using your washer (see below).

If you are very careful, you can do the above steps in your washing machine. Use the soak cycle, and add the fleece as soon as the tub is full. I cannot emphasize this enough: once the tub is full, turn the washer off. You may even need to unplug it. Many models actually agitate during their soak cycle, and

if that happens your cat's going to have a nice new felted bed (don't ask me how I know this).

When the water has cooled completely, turn the washer back on and run the spin cycle. Be sure it doesn't rinse the fleece with cold water. (Again, you need both a change in temperature and agitation in order to felt—if you make sure the temperature doesn't suddenly change, using the spin cycle isn't dangerous.) If your fleece is extra dirty, you might have to do this entire process two or even three times. They don't call this process "scouring" for nothing.

Air-dry the fleece outside on a sheet. If you have a balcony or deck railing with good air circulation, you're in luck. The fleece may dry in individual, but clean "clumps," much like its structure before taking a bath, and if this is the case, you may not even need to card it. However, carding is not only easy and fun, it can also provide some special color effects in your finished yarn if you combine different fibers.

Carding

What is carding? Carding aligns the fibers in one direction to make them easier to spin. You can use carding paddles ("handcards") or a drum carder. Either will do the job well and can be used on everything from unprocessed clean fleece to roving and top. Don't be tempted to card dirty wool—the fibers will stick together and may damage your carding apparatus.

Using Handcards

Take a small handful of fiber and lay it across one paddle with the fibers aligned vertically. This is called "charging" the handcard.

Using your dominant hand, gently sweep the second paddle across the first, as if you were combing very tangled hair.

Continue to sweep across from bottom to top of the handcard in your nondominant hand.

You will end up with roughly equal amounts of nicely aligned fiber on both paddles.

Remove the fiber by gently gathering the loose tips together in your hand and pulling them off the paddle in one motion. Some spinners roll the fiber off the paddle from side to side. No matter which method you use, what you've just created is called a "rolag."

Place the rolag aside and card another handful of fiber. When you have a nice collection of rolags assembled, you'll be ready to spin!

Charge the handcard (or paddle) by placing a layer of fiber on the teeth parallel to the short dimension of the handcard.

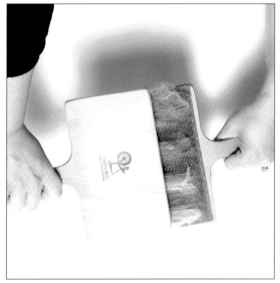

Gently sweep the second paddle across the first to align the individual fibers.

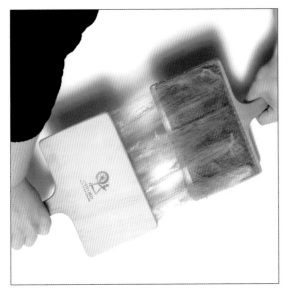

Use the paddle in your dominant hand to sweep across the other paddle several times.

When the fiber is sufficiently carded, there will be roughly equal amounts of fiber aligned on each paddle.

Gently gather the loose tips and pull the fibers off the paddle in one motion to form a rolag.

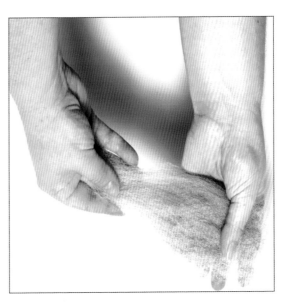

When you have a nice collection of rolags, you'll be ready to spin.

Using a Drum Carder

Drum carders automate the "sweeping" motion of the handcard method. By feeding small amounts of fiber into the intake section and turning a crank on the side, you can align the fibers around the large center cylinder. When enough fiber has accumulated, remove it using a pointed tool and your hands. Advanced color and fiber blending is possible with a drum carder—you can include glittery strands, sari silk shreds, bits of embroidery thread, or cut up wool scraps, as well as an infinite variety of other colors into the fiber mix.

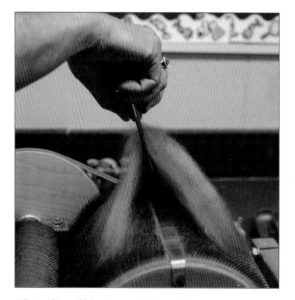

Lift the fiber off the drum with the tool supplied with the drum carder.

Drum carders produce large rolags.

Chapter 2
Spindles

Spindles are used to spin yarn by hand (i.e., without a wheel). In its most basic form, a spindle allows you to easily add twist to fiber to turn it into spun yarn, called singles. (Note that the term "singles" is used for both singular and plural applications.) As the yarn is spun, it is wrapped around the spindle for temporary storage. The yarn wrapped around a spindle is called a "cop." You can knit with individual cops of singles, or you can spin two or more cops together to make plied yarn.

Spindles have been around for tens of thousands of years. Some of the earliest spindle whorls shaped as we would recognize them date to 5000 B.C. in Middle Eastern excavations, and there are Egyptian wall paintings of hooked high-whorl spindles that date even earlier.

Even after spinning wheels became more common, spindle-spun fibers remained in demand. The spindle's portability was an asset to people on the move, not to mention its lower price (just like today). Also, fewer parts equals fewer things to

break or go wrong—and while few people would attempt to build their own wheel, making your own spindle is simple and enjoyable.

The basic parts of a spindle are the whorl, shaft, and hook. Hooks are optional; some spindles use a notch in the shaft to hold the singles while you're spinning more fiber onto it.

As far as classifying spindles into types, there are two major families: drop spindles and supported spindles, and within each family there are several different types.

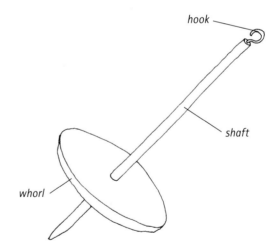

The basic parts of a spindle are the whorl, shaft, and hook. Hooks are optional; some spindles use a notch in the shaft to hold the singles while you're spinning more fiber onto it.

Drop Spindles

Don't panic. Some new spinners I've met don't like the term "drop spindle," since they associate it with dropping the spindle accidentally—not what it's designed to do, which is "drop" or "hang" in midair. I'm not saying you'll never drop the spindle while you're learning, but I can reassure you it's not a big deal. Everyone, even the most experienced spindler, will drop a drop spindle on the floor from time to time.

Bottom-whorl spindles are used for medium to long fiber. If the fiber is shorter, or if you want to spin a finer yarn, choose a spindle with a lighter-weight whorl. These spindles usually have a notch at the end of the spindle shaft to catch the yarn while you spin. They are better suited for spinning heavier yarns since they move more slowly.

Top-whorl (sometimes called high-whorl) spindles are also recommended for medium to long fiber, and for spinning medium to fine yarn. They have a small hook on top to hold the yarn while spinning. They are usually lighter in weight than a bottom-whorl spindle, and spin faster as a result.

Turkish spindles have two removeable crossbars instead of a whorl. Yarn is wound under and over the bars while spinning to create a center-pull ball.

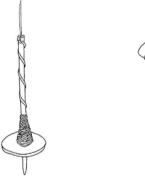

bottom-whorl spindle

top-whorl spindle

Turkish spindle

Supported Spindles

In another example of "name explains it all," supported spindles are supported by something as they spin, whether it's the spinner's leg, a cup or bowl, or even a tabletop.

If you have problems with a drop spindle but don't want to move to a wheel, try a supported spindle. My personal favorite is the takhli-style spindle. For some spinners, it's easier to control their hand motions when they're not worrying about the spindle hanging in midair. Supported spindles are also recommended for homes with devious cats. (Can you blame them? After all, it does look like a toy hanging from a string.)

Navajo spindles have a large, heavy whorl near the base of the shaft, which rests on the floor. The spindle is rolled on the spinner's leg.

Tahkli spindles are lightweight, often with a metal shaft, which is twirled in a bowl or other small container to keep the spindle point in one place.

Russian spindles (also sometimes called Orenburg lace spindles) have a long, wooden shaft with a tiny budlike whorl on the end and are used to spin very fine laceweight yarns such as the ones used in Orenburg shawls.

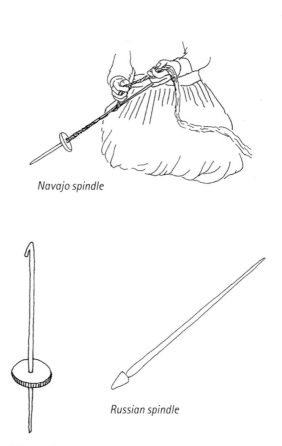

Navajo spindle

tahkli spindle

Russian spindle

Make Your Own CD Spindle

Finally, here's a way to put all those old CDs to use! Making your own spindle from a CD is not only a very satisfying project but also a clever bit of recycling.

A trip to the hardware store should yield most of the materials on this list. If you use a lot of bulk CD-Rs, you may have some of the clear "blanks" used as spacers at the top of the bulk packaging on hand. These make really fun spindles because

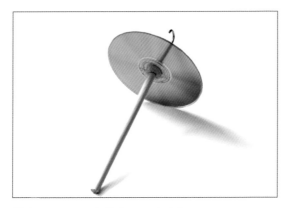

Make your own spindle from materials available at hardware stores.

You Will Need:
- two CDs
- a rubber grommet (available from bonkersfiber.com)
- ¾-inch (2 cm) hardwood dowel
- a cup hook
- a short length of plastic tubing to fit over the dowel.

you can sandwich fabric, photos, or other artwork between two clear blanks.

Trim the dowel to your preferred spindle shaft length (10–12 inches [25.5–30.5 cm] is average); most hardware stores will do this for you if you ask. Screw the cup hook into the end of your trimmed dowel. It helps to make a small pilot hole with a nail or another screw to make sure the cup hook is centered. Hold the CDs back to back and insert the rubber grommet inside the CDs' center opening. Slide a few inches of plastic tubing over your dowel, at the bottom end away from the hook for a bottom-whorl spindle, a few inches from the hook for a top whorl. Insert the dowel and its plastic sleeve into the grommet in the center of the CD. Make a tiny notch with a sharp kitchen or utility knife in the side of the CDs if your spindle is top whorl (your already-spun singles will rest in this notch as you spin more). That's all. These make great gifts for other spinners or knitters you'd like to "convert."

How to Choose a Spindle

So many spinners start off with a CD spindle—if you've mastered yours, you may want to try something new. Think about what kind of yarn you like to spin, or more broadly, the types of things you like to knit. Weavers may want to try a Navajo spindle with Churro wool, as traditional Navajo weavers use. Lace knitters could try spinning some fine laceweight merino on a top whorl. Chunky yarn lovers can use a Turkish spindle to form their own center-pull ball as they spin. As with any craft, having the right tools makes the job easier.

Make Your Own Spindle Lazy Kate

You don't have to juggle multiple spindles if you want to create a multi-ply yarn. It's possible to spin and ply multiple cops of singles together using just one spindle and a little craftiness by building your own lazy kate. Lazy kates are used by wheel spinners to hold bobbins full of singles. They allow the bobbins to spin on an axis and feed two or more singles into the spinner's hand for plying.

To make your own lazy kate, purchase the items listed in the box below. Screw the cup hook into the wood burning blank as shown in the photograph. Hammer two or three nails (or screw in screws) evenly spaced in the blank; hammer in only enough to keep them upright—about ¾ inch (2 cm). Voilà, you have a basic lazy kate! Before you spin, insert your spindle shaft into a straw. If your spindle is too big for the straw, simply wrap some stiff paper around the shaft and tape it down. Wind your singles over the straw or paper wrap. When you're done spinning, the straw (or paper) can be removed from the spindle, along with the newly spun yarn (the cop).

To use your kate, slip an empty straw over a nail, then insert the tip of your spindle's shaft into the empty straw. (If you're using the paper method, detailed above, slide the singles and their paper core over the straw or directly over the nail.) Slide the spun singles down onto the straw standing on the lazy kate. Repeat for each spindle. Run the ends under the cup hook, which will help tension the yarn as you ply it. Place the kate on the floor, and attach the ends of each single to your leader. Spin. If you spun the singles clockwise, you will want to ply counterclockwise, and vice versa.

A traditional lazy kate holds multiple bobbins of wheel-spun singles for plying.

You Will Need:
- a wood burning blank (craft stores sell these in precut plaque shapes; buy one at least an inch thick)
- a brass cup hook
- drinking straws
- the longest "headless" finish nails you can find (screws will also work if you can fit their top inside the straws)

Make your own lazy kate from a wood burning blank, cup hook, and a couple of nails.

Ply the yarn from two cops of singles.

Chapter 3

Wheels

Are you trapped in a fairy tale? No, it's just a diagram of various spinning wheel parts, although the names definitely sound like something out of the Brothers Grimm. Footman, maidens, mother-of-all. . . .

Axle: the center shaft of the drive wheel

Bobbin: a spool that gathers yarn as it is spun

Brake: a tensioning device on some wheels that allows the bobbin to spin slower or faster than the flyer so the yarn will wind on smoothly

Crank: a part that connects the axle and footman to turn the drive wheel's axle

Drive band: a cord connecting the drive wheel with bobbin or flyer

Drive wheel: a large wheel that turns the spindle or flyer

Flyer: the U-shaped device that guides yarn onto the bobbin

Footman: a vertical bar or string which connects the treadle and crank

Maidens: a pair of upright bars that hold the bobbin

Mother-of-all: the horizontal section that holds the maidens and various tensioning devices

Orifice: the tube or metal triangle where the yarn feeds through to the flyer

Tension knob: a device that controls brake or drive-band tension

Treadle: a foot pedal that turns the drive wheel

Whorl: a groove at the end of a bobbin that holds the drive or brake band

While a spinning wheel has many more parts than a spindle, it operates in roughly the same way. Your foot, by pressing down on the treadle, causes the footman (or footmen, if you have a double-treadle wheel) to move the crank, placing the drive wheel's axle (and therefore, the wheel itself) in motion. Sounds complicated, but it's actually only the wheel equivalent of flicking your spindle with

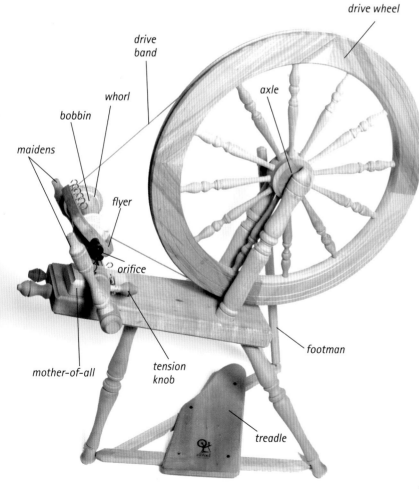

drive wheel

drive band

whorl

axle

bobbin

maidens

flyer

orifice

footman

mother-of-all

tension knob

treadle

one hand to get it turning. You still need to draft the fiber and feed it to the device. The difference is that the spun fiber isn't wound directly onto a spindle shaft for storage, but passes through the orifice and winds onto a bobbin.

Flyers

The basic mechanics of all wheels are the same except for the flyer type, which controls how the yarn is guided onto the bobbin. (Flyers and bobbins have to travel at slightly different speeds in order for the yarn to wind on.) Until you've been spinning for a while, you probably won't have a flyer preference. If you choose to try out several wheels before purchasing one, though, note what types of flyer each uses. Your personal spinning style may point you more toward one type than another. There are many different flyer/bobbin combinations: the three most common are listed below.

Single-band, flyer-lead (Scotch tension): Bobbins have a separate, adjustable brake to control the speed of yarn draw-in, so the bobbin slows while the flyer rotates more quickly, winding on the yarn.

Single-band, bobbin-lead: There is a drive band on the bobbin and a brake on the flyer. The flyer slows while the bobbin continues to rotate more quickly, which winds on the yarn.

Double-drive, bobbin-lead: A single band goes around the drive wheel twice, once around the bobbin and once around the flyer. The bobbin spins faster than the flyer, winding on the yarn.

Wheel Types

There are also many different types of wheels; if possible, try out several before choosing one. You may also have space concerns. When I lived in a single-room studio, I owned a small, portable wheel much like the one pictured below, which is even smaller, as it folds flat into a traveling case. Now that I have more space, I have added a traditional wheel to my collection. But is it really "traditional"? This style may be what first comes to mind when spinning wheels are mentioned; however, for as long as there have been spinning wheels, there have been different types of wheels: upright, Saxony, great wheel, castle wheel—even electric spinners and wheels built from PVC pipe. You're only constrained by the amount of space you have and price you want to pay.

Many portable wheels fold flat and fit into a carrying case.

Chapter 4

Getting Started

It pays to take time up front to prepare your fiber. I know it's tempting to dive right in, but the actual spinning goes more smoothly if your fiber is prepared well. Most beginners start out using top, which is quite compressed. If you try to spin directly from the top without predrafting (fluffing) it, more effort is required to pull out the fibers and feed them onto your spindle or wheel. The same goes for many other types of fiber, with the exception of sliver or very thin pencil roving. It will also be more difficult to control the amount of twist you are adding to the singles, and if you're yanking on the top, it's easy to get distracted as you treadle or allow your spindle to spin.

YOU WILL LEARN:
- The basic mechanics of spinning, with both drop spindles and wheels.
- What to expect when you begin, i.e., "lumpy-bumpy" yarn is your friend.
- Easy ways to "unlump" yarn, such as running it back through the wheel to remove twist.
- Controlling what kind of singles you produce—what happens when you pinch this way or pull that way.
- Twist—S and Z, how they affect the yarn and what you do.
- Plying—to take out overtwist, even out lumps, do interesting things with color.

A "singles" is the strand of twisted fiber that results from spinning. Plied with another singles, or two or three, it becomes yarn—although you may also choose to leave it unplied and knit with it as a singles yarn.

Before You Spin

Start with a manageable length of fiber: 12–18 inches (30.5–45.5 cm). The way you prepare a multicolor roving for spinning has a strong effect on the finished appearance of yarn made from it (see Lynne Vogel's *The Twisted Sisters Sock Workbook* for

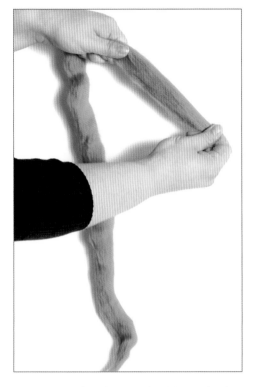

Hold the end of the fiber tightly with your dominant hand and the rest about 6 inches (15 cm) away in your other hand. Give the fiber a quick tug.

A section of fiber will separate off into your dominant hand.

This section will be the average staple length.

more on this). You can split the roving lengthwise or divide it where the colors change—in fact, there are many different options. But no matter how you divide it, the first step is to open up, or predraft, the fiber. This makes the actual drafting easier.

First, determine the average staple length in the fiber you are using.

Grasp the end of the fiber sample tightly with your dominant hand, gently holding the rest about 6 inches (15 cm) away in your other hand. Give the fiber a hard, quick tug. A section will separate off into your dominant hand; measuring this should give you an idea of the average staple length. Let's assume it is 4 inches (10 cm).

Now that you know the staple length, you can begin "predrafing." Predrafting will open up the fiber and make the actual drafting for spinning on a wheel or spindle. Working from one side of the fiber to the other and from the top down to the bottom, pull a piece of the carded fiber apart into a wide, flat horizontal section. You want the fiber to become more open, but not to separate into smaller pieces.

When you reach the end, begin pulling the fiber out vertically. Keeping your hands farther apart

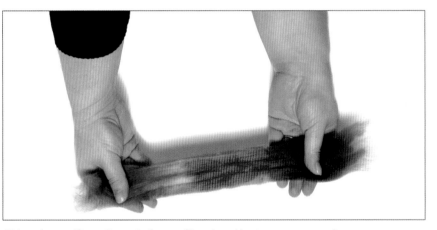

Although you will usually predraft more fiber than this at once, use a small piece to experiment with these instructions.

Working from one side of the fiber to the other and from top to bottom, pull the piece apart into a wide, flat rectangular shape.

than the staple length and pulling slowly with consistent tension will cause the individual fibers to glide past each other without separating into multiple sections.

What began as a short, thick section of top will now be longer and thinner. Ideally, you will be able to see through the fiber if you held it in front of your eyes. Now you're ready to spin!

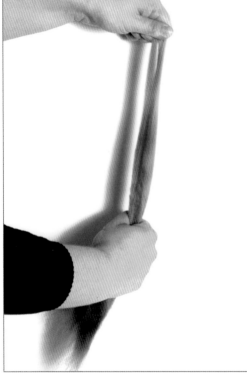

Pull vertically to cause the individual fibers to glide past one another.

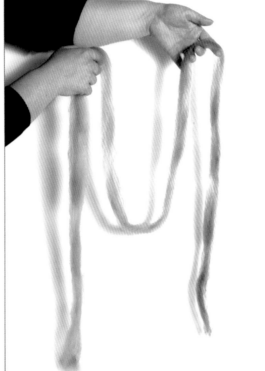

What began as a short, thick section of fiber will now be much longer and thinner.

The Basic Mechanics of Spindles and Wheels

Both spindles and wheels do the same thing: they add twist to drafted fiber. But there are differences in the way they do this. Spindles operate in an upright position—the fiber is held vertically, and twist is added. Wheels take in the fiber horizontally. Another difference is how the twist is added—spindles are rotated using a flick of the wrist, and wheels are "pedaled" much like a bike, using one or two treadles. But there is absolutely no difference in the end product. Some spinners say they can spin faster with a wheel, some say a spindle is faster.

For example, I find wheel spinning easier due to a permanent elbow injury that makes it difficult for me to hold up my arm for long periods of time. If you have physical considerations such as problems with your ankles or wrists, you may want to try both methods before settling on one. There are even electric spinners that don't involve treadling at all.

Start Spindling!

To start spinning with a spindle, you must have "leader" on your spindle. The leader should be a piece of yarn about 18 inches (45.5 cm) long; preferably wool (it will help "grab" the loose fiber better than a smooth yarn). Tie the leader on to the spindle shaft and wrap the yarn around the shaft several times.

Wrap the leader several times around the spindle shaft.

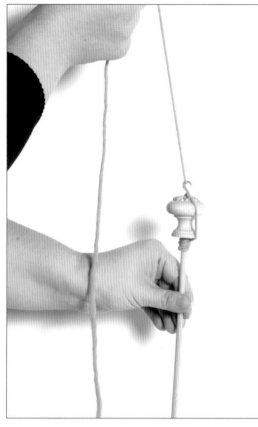

Rest the leader yarn in the notch on the side of the spindle (if there is one) and wrap the yarn around the hook once or twice; there should be several inches of leader yarn above the hook.

Slip the leader under the hook (pictured here on top of the spindle; some spindles feature a whorl on the bottom and a notch at the top; see page 22). The whorl, which is the solid, usually round piece on a spindle, provides needed weight to make the spindle spin longer.

You may have a small notch cut into the side of your whorl. If so, rest the yarn in that notch and wrap the leader around the hook once or twice. You should now have several inches of the leader extending above the hook. Place the spindle aside for a moment.

Wrap some of your previously drafted fiber around the wrist of your nondominant hand, leaving about 12 inches (30.5 cm) loose and hanging between your forefinger and thumb. If you have a wrist distaff, which will help keep the fiber in place without slipping (think of it as a bracelet-style holder for fiber; see page 47), now's the time to put it on. Pick up the spindle by the loose end of the leader, using your dominant hand.

Overlap the last few inches of the leader onto the end of the fiber and wrap the fiber around it. If your leader were a hot dog, the fiber would be the bun.

Keep pinching the "hot dog" together with your fiber hand and start spinning the spindle with your dominant hand. You can spin clockwise or counterclockwise, but whichever you pick, be consistent or you will undo the twist in your spun yarn.

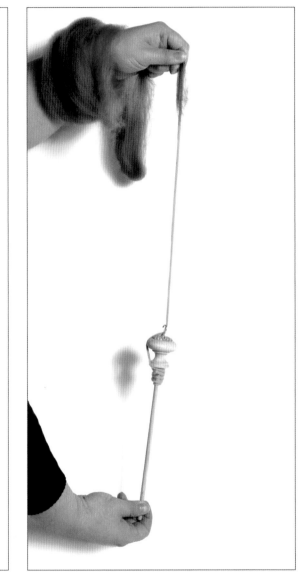

Wrap the previously drafted fiber around the wrist of your nondominant hand, leaving about 12 inches loose and hanging between the forefinger and thumb.

Pinch the fiber around the top of the leader to hold it in place as you begin to spin the spindle.

As the spindle begins to twist the fiber around the leader, gently pull new fiber down from above, a little at a time. Concentrate on pulling it out evenly, although it will probably be a little lumpy at first.

When the spindle slows, give it another flick with your hand to set it spinning in the same direction again. Once you have a few feet of twisted fiber, stop, pinch the fiber where the twist ends with your fiber hand, and hold the spindle shaft.

Unhook the leader or spun yarn from the top of the spindle and wind it onto the spindle shaft. Place the yarn back around the hook and start spinning again. That's all there is to it!

If you break the fiber, you will repeat the "hot dog" pinching process to make another join, repeating the instructions above until the new fiber has joined on to the yarn still connected to the spindle. If you feel the spindle is going too quickly, or that you are not in control of the fiber, don't hesitate to step on the "brake" by putting the spindle shaft between your knees. Hold it still while you adjust your fiber or hands. As you become more skilled, you'll notice that standing up while spindling means you can spin longer without having to wind on. I've even seen Laura Jefferson (see page 90) spin over her stair railing, half a floor above her studio floor so she could spin longer lengths of yarn without stopping to wind on.

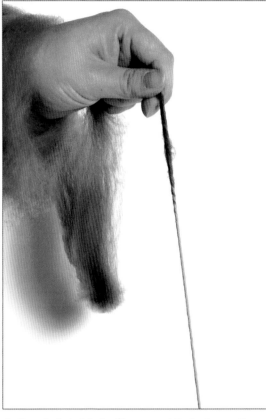

As the spindle twists the fiber around the leader, gently pull new fiber down from above, a little at a time.

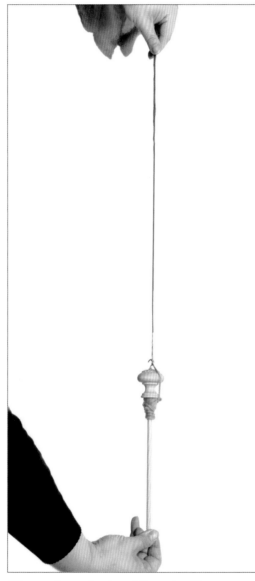

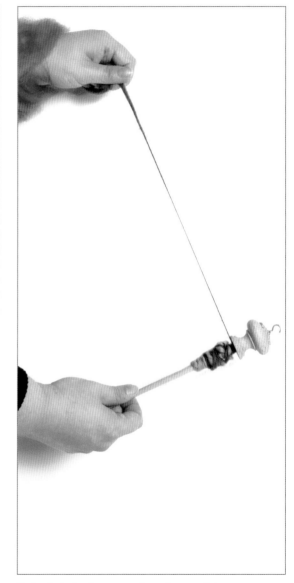

When you have a few feet of fiber twisted into yarn, stop, hold the spindle shaft with your nonfiber hand, and use your fiber hand to pinch the fiber where the twist ends.

Unhook the leader or yarn from the top of the spindle and wind it onto the spindle shaft.

Wheel Spinning

If you've mastered the spindle, chances are you will find spinning on a wheel very simple. Whenever possible, I recommend learning on a spindle first, because things go more slowly and it gives you a chance to really observe what's going on. It's also easier to eliminate overtwisting as you go along on a spindle, though I will show you how to correct this and other common wheel problems shortly. Here's how to get started on a wheel:

As in the spindling instructions, tie a leader on to your bobbin and wrap it around the bobbin a few times in a clockwise direction.

Guide the leader around one or two of the flyer hooks and, using the orifice hook (if your wheel didn't come with one, you can improvise with a paper clip), pull the leader through.

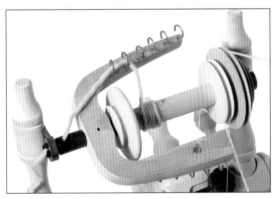

Guide the leader around one or two of the flyer hooks and through the orifice.

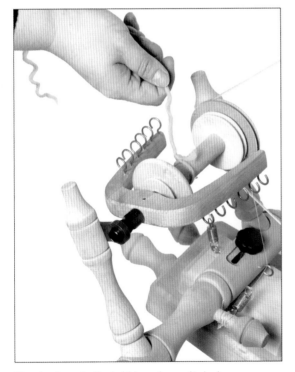

Tie a leader onto the bobbin and wrap it clockwise around the bobbin a few times.

The photograph below shows how to use the orifice hook to thread the leader:

The leader is through and running across 2 flyer hooks. You should have at least 12 inches (30.5 cm) of yarn leader between the orifice and your hands.

Wrap your previously drafted fiber around the end of the leader and pinch the two together. Hold on tightly and start to treadle your wheel in a clockwise direction.

Momentarily, the twist will reach the pinching fingers of your fiber hand and the fiber will start to

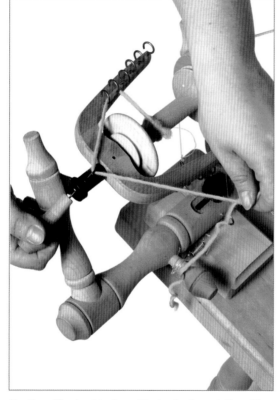

Use the orifice hook to thread the leader through the orifice.

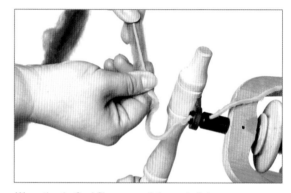

Wrap the drafted fiber around the end of the leader and pinch the two together.

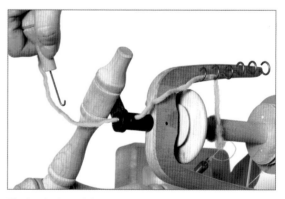

The leader is positioned correctly around the flyer hooks and through the orifice.

grasp the leader. As soon as they've become "glued" together, let go and allow the twisted fiber to start winding through the wheel orifice and onto the bobbin.

While this is happening, begin drawing the fiber out of your "fiber hand" by pinching it gently with your dominant hand and pulling. This is where all your fiber preparation work will pay off.

As you continue to treadle, and pull out new fiber from your supply, the twist will travel into the new fiber as it moves toward its new home on the bobbin.

Fixing a break in the fiber is easy. If you didn't catch the loose end in time, unwind it from the bobbin and thread about 12 inches (30.5 cm) back out the orifice. Hold the two ends side by side.

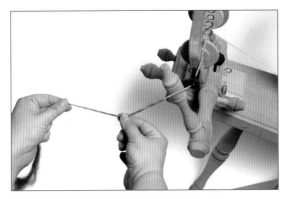

Treadling the wheel will cause the fiber to twist and grasp the leader.

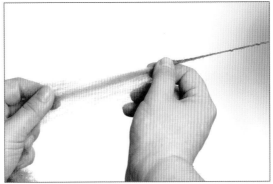

Draw the fiber out of your fiber hand by pinching it gently with your dominant hand and pulling away.

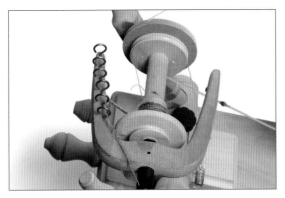

The fiber will wrap onto the bobbin.

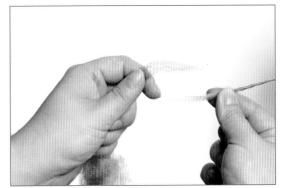

To fix a break in the fiber, hold the two ends side by side, pinch them together, and start treadling.

Pinch them together and start treadling. As the two fibers become entwined, let go and allow the joined area to move through the orifice and onto the bobbin. If you have a tough time with this, practice using two different colors of fiber (one on the bobbin, one in your hand). It's easier to determine whether the ends are entwined enough.

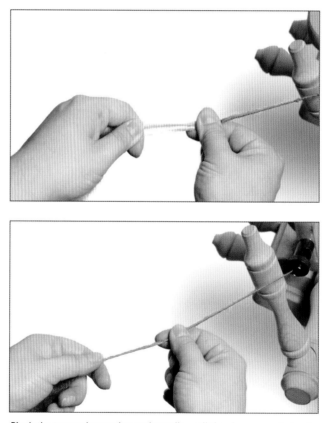

Pinch the two ends together and treadle until they become entwined.

Common Problems

If the fiber is over-twisted and kinks up before it even reaches the orifice, treadle more slowly.

If the fiber breaks frequently, you may not be treadling enough.

If the fiber does not "take up" onto the bobbin, your leader may have unwound or the yarn may be caught on one of the flyer hooks.

If you're having other problems, the tension on your wheel may be set incorrectly. If you can't correct this problem using your wheel's manual, this is where a wheel-savvy friend or shop owner comes in handy. If it is difficult to treadle, or the wheel squeals, it may need to be oiled. There are many more variables to juggle when spinning on a wheel instead of a spindle, but the overall gain in speed is worth it, in my opinion.

If the fiber is over-twisted and kinks up before it reaches the orifice, treadle more slowly.

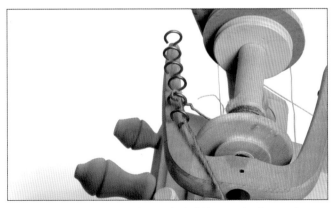

If the fiber does not "take up" onto the bobbin, your leader may have unwound or the yarn may be caught on one of the flyer hooks.

The flyer hooks on the wheel control where the singles winds on to the bobbin. As you begin to fill one section of the bobbin, you will need to pause and move the singles over a hook or two. To fit the maximum yardage on your bobbin, move the singles to a new flyer hook frequently to fill the bobbin evenly. Start with the leader in the hook farthest away from you if you want to see more easily when it's time to move down a hook.

If you accidentally treadle in the reverse direction, you won't get far—the yarn will tangle on the bobbin. If this happens, let go of the fiber and gently unwind it from the flyer hooks near the bobbin, as well as anything else it may have caught on in the process. Pull on the end near your fiber supply until the singles is once again taut and ready to wind on. You may need to put a little more twist into the fiber before you let it wind back onto the bobbin, and proceed as usual.

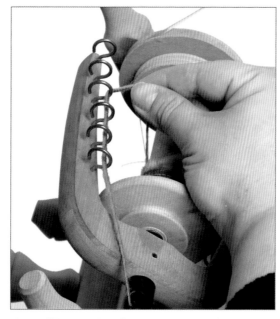

As you fill one section of the bobbin, move the single over a hook or two to direct it to another part of the bobbin.

If you treadle in the reverse direction, you'll soon have a tangle.

Tips and Tricks

No matter what spinning equipment you use, heavy yarn needs fewer twists per inch to hold together than fine yarn, and shorter fibers need more twist than long ones. Knowing your average staple length (see page 29) will help you adapt your spinning or treadling speed.

There are many different ways of drafting fiber and different methods yield different characteristics in the singles you create. The method described above is a simple version of the "inchworm" drafting method. The spinner pinches and feeds smaller sections of fiber into the drafting zone (the triangle between the hand holding the fiber supply and where the twist enters the fibers), using the dominant hand's fingers to smooth over the singles while moving backward to pull out more fiber.

If you're spinning with long fibers or from a batt, you may also want to try "spinning from the fold." Pull off a staple length's worth of fiber and fold it in half. Hold it so that it is folded around the index and/or middle finger of your fiber hand and pull the fibers from the middle "fold" section instead of the end. Continue to pull fiber from the fold instead of the ends as you spin.

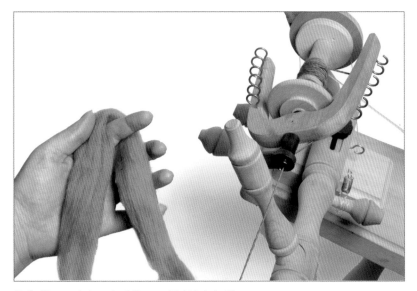

Pull off a staple length of fiber and fold it in half.

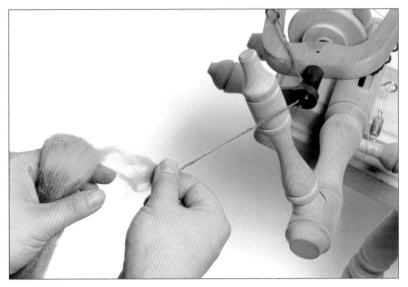

Pull the fibers from the middle of the fold.

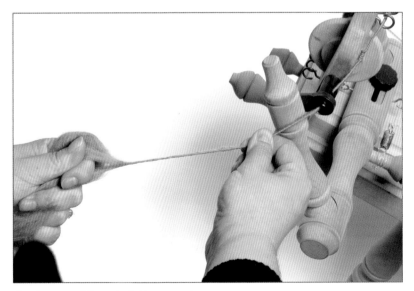

Continue to pull from the fold as you spin.

Twisty Dilemmas

There are two types of twist in yarn. Z-twist is created when the singles is spun clockwise; S-twist is created when the singles is spun

counterclockwise. Most plied handspun is made from two Z-twisted singles spun together using an S-twist. Regardless of the twist's direction, too much twist is probably one of the most common problems for new spinners. To remove excess twist, stop treadling or spin-

ning the spindle, draft out a bit more fiber, and let the twist distribute itself over a longer distance. It's the equivalent of adding water to a too-salty soup: by giving the single a little more "volume," the excess twist is diluted.

If you have large unintentional slubs (chunks of lightly spun fiber) or thick sections, stop, grasp the section in question and untwist it manually with your fingers, then gently elongate it. Allow the twist to run in to the unspun section. You can also treadle a few revolutions in the opposite direction, then feed the singles back on. If you have an entire bobbin that's too twisty, wind it back onto a second bobbin (going slowly in the opposite direction) to remove some of the twist.

Ply Me a River

Whether using a spindle or wheel, as soon as your spindle shaft or bobbin is full, you will need to take the singles off before you can use them. If you don't plan to ply your singles, you can wind directly onto a niddy-noddy. If you want to ply them with a

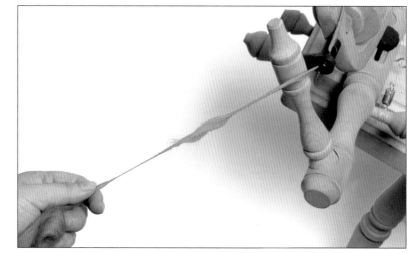

Untwist an area of thick or lightly spun fibers manually with your fingers, then gently elongate it.

second strand, set the bobbin aside, or wind the spindle's contents off onto a storage bobbin.

Don't have two full bobbins or spindles? Want to see what the yarn would look like plied before you spin some more? Try one of the following three methods:

Center-pull Ball

Wind the singles into a center-pull ball. Hold both the outside and inside strands together, attach them to the leader, and start plying. It's helpful to hold the lower part of the center-pull ball with your nondominant hand to keep some tension on the ball and prevent it from moving around too much.

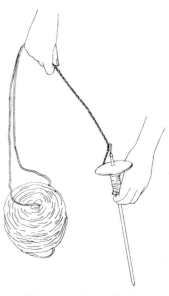

Ply the outside and inside strands of a center-pull ball.

Andean Plying

Andean plying is probably my favorite one-bobbin-or-less plying method. In this method, your wrist acts as a nøstepinne. Start with the palm of your nondominant hand facing you (the left hand is shown here). Pinch the yarn end between your thumb and forefinger, then take it across the back of your hand to the wrist at the base of your little

finger. Turn your hand so the back of your hand is facing you. *Pass the yarn across the palm side of your wrist to the base of your thumb. Take the yarn up the back of your hand, between your ring and middle fingers, around the middle finger, and back to the base of your thumb. Bring the yarn back across the palm side of your wrist to the base of your little finger. Take the yarn up the back of your

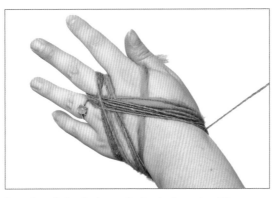

Loosely pull the singles up the back of your hand from the little finger side, between your middle and forefinger, around the middle finger, back to the little finger side of the wrist, and across the palm side to the base of your thumb.

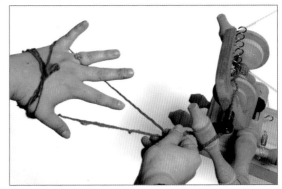

With a little practice, you'll learn how to rotate your wrist to release the singles into the plying zone.

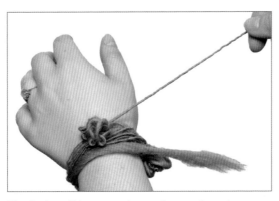

The singles will be wrapped around your wrist and there will be two ends of yarn to work with.

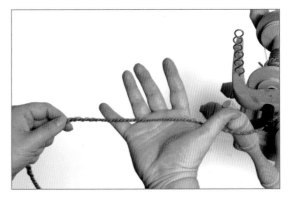

Andean-ply a small amount of yarn to see what it looks like before you begin to spin a whole batch.

hand, between your middle and forefinger, around the middle finger, and back to the base of your little finger. Repeat from * until the singles runs out, wrapping as loosely as possible so you don't cut off the circulation in your middle finger.

Pinching both yarn ends between your thumb and forefinger, ease your middle finger out of the loops and let the loops fall to the back of your hand. Slide the wrapped singles down to your wrist while continuing to hold the two yarn ends.

Attach the ends to the leader and start to ply. With a little practice, you'll learn how to swivel your wrist to release the singles easily into the plying zone. It almost looks like you're dancing the hula from the elbow down.

Andean plying comes in handy when you're spinning a small amount of yarn and want to see what it looks like before committing to spinning and plying a larger amount.

Navajo Plying

Navajo plying is useful when you're working with a multicolor roving and want to keep the individual colors distinct in the final, plied yarn. Attach the singles to your bobbin leader and make a slipknot. Hold the sides of the slipknot opening apart with one thumb and forefinger. Insert your other thumb and forefinger into the loop, catch the singles coming from the bobbin, and draw it through the loop to create a long new loop. While you're doing all that, keep spinning or treadling. I've heard other spinners compare the basic construction to crochet, in that the loops are interconnected. Think of your fingers as the hook—you're basically making a chain stitch.

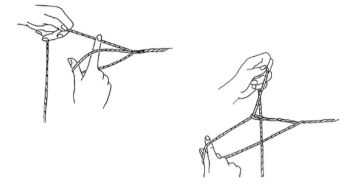

For Navajo plying, hold the sides of the slipknot opening apart with one thumb and forefinger, then insert your other thumb and forefinger to draw up a new loop of singles through the old loop.

MAKE YOUR OWN WRIST DISTAFF

Now that you've learned how to ply, you can make your own wrist distaff. Sandy Sitzman (see page 119), who makes gorgeous distaffs, taught me the following method. Make a cabled yarn by plying two 2-ply yarns together. Your cabled yarn should be long enough to wrap loosely around your wrist with enough space to slip easily over your hand, plus several extra inches that will hang down. Tie an overhand knot where the fit is best, leaving the tails hanging. At this point you can add beads, extra yarn, tassels, or any other decoration to the yarn ends. To use the distaff, slip it on like a bracelet and wind your fiber loosely around the dangling ends to keep it out of the way while you spindle. It's often easier to release fiber from a distaff than to unwind it from your wrist.

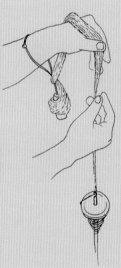

A loop of yarn slipped over your wrist makes a simple distaff.

Finishing Yarn—or "My Niddy-noddy is Full, Now What?"

To go from niddy-noddy (see page 8) to knit-table, there are a few more things you need to do. Fortunately, they're all simple and one of them is especially stress-relieving!

First, while the yarn is still on the niddy-noddy, take some waste yarn and tie off sections in figure eights by dividing the yarn down the middle with your finger and threading the waste yarn through in an "8" as shown below before tying it firmly. Tie at least one figure eight per niddy section (four ties total).

If you know your yarn is a little overtwisted, you can damp-block it while it's still on the niddy and allow it to dry before you remove it. Otherwise, take the skein off your niddy and soak it in water with a gentle cleanser (treat it as if you were washing any handknit, being careful not to change water temperatures drastically or agitate too much).

Here's where it gets fun. In order to "set the twist," whack the damp skein against a solid surface. Tiled shower walls are perfect, as are balcony railings and flagpoles. Hold the skein firmly at one end and slap the skein against the surface until little or no water flies out. Then hang the skein to dry and weight the end with something.

When the skein is dry, you can twist it into a hank (like commercial yarn) for storage, or wind it into a ball and knit it right away.

To wind a skein for storage, place your hands in the center of the loop forming the skein, twist your wrists in opposite directions to twist the skein, then pull the loop that's wrapped around one wrist through the loop on the other, and allow the skein to twist back on itself.

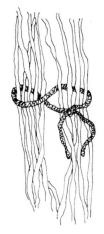

Tie off yarn on the niddy with figure-eight ties.

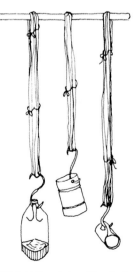

Weight the skein with a just about any household item.

"M-O-T-H" and Other Four-letter Words

After all the love and attention you lavish on your handspun, why risk moth infestation? Here are some herbs and aromatics that make a moth-repelling potpourri. Mix some (or all) of these ingredients together and protect your precious yarn: balsam fir, cedar, geranium, pennyroyal, sweet marjoram, tarragon, bay, cinnamon, lavender, rosemary, sweet woodruff, wormwood, cloves, tansy.

If you'd like to commemorate your very first skein, why not knit one or both sides of a sachet from it? Fill the sachet with herbs (refreshing occasionally with essential oils) and you may never have to say that four-letter word again.

To wind a skein for storage, twist the skein on itself then tuck one end into the other.

Protect your yarn with a mixture of aromatic herbs.

Chapter 5

Handspun from a Knitter's Perspective

Handspun yarn is not commercial yarn. I will repeat this more than once throughout the book, particularly when introducing knitting uses for handspun yarns. Your first yarns will be uneven, they will be "lumpy bumpy" and they will not resemble anything you can buy in a store—not at first, anyway. But this is a good thing: almost every spinning teacher will tell you to save the first yarn you ever make because "you will never be able to do it that way again." This is absolutely true. A new spinner I know decided to call her first efforts "designer" yarn, which has since become my preferred term for that unusual stuff that comes off the first spindle or bobbin.

What if you don't want to make "designer" yarn? Take heart—there are ways to fix even the twistiest problem. And chances are, overtwist will be the worst problem you will face as a new spinner. Here are some strategies to conquer it.

Energized Singles

"Energized" singles are knitted right off the bobbin or spindle and maintain a high amount of twist. They twist sideways, even in plain stockinette stitch. Wait just two or three days and the tendency

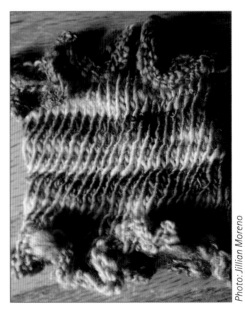

Photo: Jillian Moreno

This wristlet, spun and knit by Jillian Moreno, shows how much energized singles can bias to one side.

- Ply two singles together. The overtwist in each individual singles will cancel each other out. If you only have one bobbin or spindle's worth, try Andean plying (see page 46).
- Run the yarn back through your wheel in the opposite direction. If you spun clockwise, go counterclockwise and vice versa. But be careful not to untwist too much. *Note:* I have found it is much easier to overtwist if you learn on a wheel. If you're using a spindle, unwind a section of yarn, secure the yarn in the spindle's hook, and allow the spindle to drop, holding the upper end of the yarn in your hand. The weight of the spindle and its tendency to spin in the opposite direction from the twist in the yarn will take out some of the excess twist. As you complete each section of yarn, wind it onto a niddy-noddy, bobbin, or a second spindle.
- Tightly wind the singles onto a niddy-noddy and get them soaking wet. Leave the skein to dry completely on the niddy, or you'll have a curly mess. This works best on singles that are only a little overtwisted.
- Wait. If you don't need to ply or knit with the singles right away, leave them on the bobbin or spindle for several days. Sometimes singles that aren't terribly overtwisted will "set" by themselves over time.
- None of the above—use the energized singles as the designer yarn that it is.

of the yarn to bias is likely to diminish (unless the yarn was extra-overtwisted, and then it can take longer). Once the singles has been knitted, though, the twist will stay put. See the Power Station Hat on page 89 for a simple energized singles project.

The upper shoulder area in my very first handspun sweater was so energized that the sideways stockinette Vs slouched like horizontal purl stitches. Years later, the stitches have mellowed and improved their posture. If you'd like to see some other examples of energized singles used in knitting, check out the work of Kathryn Alexander and Lynne Vogel, the two best-known spinner/knitters who incorporate energized singles in their work.

Playing with Plying

Have you ever noticed that stockinette stitch knitted in commercial yarn can look different, depending on the yarn used? For example, one side of the V may be wider or angled differently from its twin. This is because each yarn's plying type affects the final appearance and drape of the knitted fabric. As a spinner, you should be familiar with various types of plying, both commercial and by hand.

Most commercial yarns are spun as very thin singles or 2-ply yarns meant for machine knitting. To meet the needs of handknitters, these singles are then plied together in various configurations to create different weights of yarn. Two birds, one stone.

A common configuration of commercial hand knitting yarns is 4-ply S-twist yarn. There are exceptions, such as Brown Sheep's Lamb's Pride (see the Laurabelle Swedish Heart shrug on page 74), which is a thick, Z-twisted singles. Close examination of the knitted fabric reveals that the right side of each stockinette V lines up in an extended vertical stripe, a characteristic of singles spun with Z-twist. It's still stockinette, it just looks slightly different than a 4-ply S-twist yarn would.

Cabled yarns, in which S-twisted singles are wrapped around each other and then plied using Z-twist, display a particular evenness on either side of the stockinette V. Multistrand yarns (6- and 8-ply or higher) are also usually S-twisted. For more details check out Michele Lock's article "Why Ply? [and how!]" in the Fall 2005 issue of Knitty.com.

Why should this matter to you? Because plying affects the character of your yarn almost as much as the method you use to create each individual singles.

Z-twist singles create exaggerated vertical lines when knitted in stockinette stitch.

Chapter 6

Color and Other Embellishments

Color. Beads. Thread. "Multimedia." If you can coax it into staying put, there aren't many limits to what you can put into your yarn. Many different elements can be used to add visual interest.

You Will Need:

- Roving
- Dye—this method works best with acid dyes, but you can also use cake dye or any other very strong liquid dye (see Resources on page 127)
- One 6–8 oz plastic bottle with nozzle top (hair coloring bottles from a beauty supply shop are ideal) for each dye color
- One 2–3 gallon stockpot with a lid that will fit upright on the bottom rack of your dishwasher
- A metal colander or steamer insert that fits inside the pot
- Plastic wrap
- Gallon- or quart-sized zippered plastic storage bags (optional)
- Newspaper
- White vinegar (full strength) in a spray bottle
- A dishwasher

Color

Color is the most obvious means of altering a plain fiber. Whether you dye unspun roving or finished yarn, you can achieve effects not found on any store shelf, and like spinning itself, you don't need expensive supplies. I prefer to dye roving because, depending on how I prepare it for spinning, I can achieve infinite color variations.

Dishwasher Dyeing

I'll admit it. I developed this technique because I'm lazy and I don't like lots of cleanup. But the effects are spectacular—the yarn used to knit the hat on the cover of this very book was dyed by the dishwasher method.

Place the roving in the large pot filled with cold or room-temperature water. Gently push the roving under the water and leave it to soak until it absorbs as much water as possible. Be careful not to agitate the roving or you may end up felting it. While the roving is soaking, cover your workspace with newspaper (the more, the better), then cover the newspaper with plastic wrap, overlapping the edges—more overlaps will ensure less leaking in the dyepot, so be generous.

Prepare the dye mixtures in the bottle(s) following manufacturer's instructions. I'm not very scientific—I tend to mix dye with a small amount of water until it "looks" strong enough. If you use this method, err on the side of caution—you can always add more dye powder if the solution is too weak, but it's hard to add enough water to dilute an overly strong mixture.

When the roving is thoroughly saturated, remove it from the pot and hold it over the sink to drain off excess water. Spread out the damp roving on top of the plastic wrap, exposing as much surface area as possible. Starting with the lightest color and progressing to the darkest, squirt the dye solution on the roving. Keep in mind that where dye is concerned, less is more. Unless the colors are all in the same family or unless you want a rainbow effect, more than four or five colors can be visually overwhelming. Don't worry if some spots of dye look small—the color in the spot will be stretched out as the fiber is drafted and spun.

When you're happy with the dye application, squirt vinegar over the entire roving. The acid in the vinegar will help the dye "strike," or grab on to the fiber. Don't worry about getting too much vinegar on the wool—in this case, more is better.

Cover the roving with another layer of plastic wrap. Roll it up like a sausage, preventing the separate sections of color from touching each other as much as possible. Wrap the entire "sausage" tightly with another layer of plastic wrap. For extra insurance against leakage, place the whole packet into a zippered storage bag.

Place the colander in the bottom of the metal pot, place the fiber packet in the colander, and place the lid on the pot. Place the pot in your dishwasher, on top of a cookie sheet if necessary to keep the pot upright. Run the dishwasher on the longest, hottest cycle possible—the steam and heat created in the pot will encourage the roving to soak

up the dye. Peek inside the pot to see if the colors have merged into each other—they should go from very spotted to blended. If necessary, run the pot through another cycle of the dishwasher. Leave the pot inside the dishwasher until it cools down.

Next comes the messy part that's best done outdoors or in a laundry sink. Remove the pot from the dishwasher and unwrap the packet. Pour off the extra dye (some will run off and gather in the package and the pot) into the sink. Fill the pot with clean water that's about the same temperature as the roving itself and gently rinse the fiber, being careful not to inadvertently felt it. The water temperature is important—if it's much hotter or colder than the fiber, the shock will probably felt the fiber. Some dye should rinse off, but most should hold tight to the fiber. Hang the fiber until completely dry. Depending on the weather and your particular living situation, you can hang it outside, above your kitchen or laundry sink, or above a stack of newspapers. Don't hang it above carpet or any other surface that could be stained by dripping dye.

Beads

Beads are probably one of the simplest additions: you can thread them onto a singles before plying or you can thread them on a fine string (or sewing thread) and spin the thread along with a singles.

Other Objects

Spinning other objects into your yarn, such as the daisies in the May Day Hat on page 85, is also relatively simple.

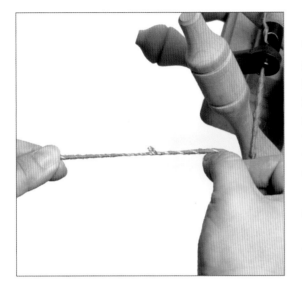

A clear bead has been threaded onto chartreuse embroidery thread for contrast, then surrounded by fiber and spun.

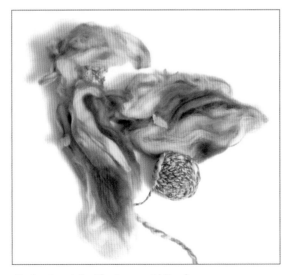

Pack rats, rejoice! Saving small bits of yarn or fiber to incorporate into future projects can help you create truly unique yarns.

Tie a few inches of yarn around the object. If you'd like the tie to blend seamlessly into the background yarn, spin your own tie from singles of the same yarn. When you're ready to add the object, slow down, wrap the drafted fiber around one end of the tie as if you were doing a join, then spin in the other side. As long as the fiber wraps around the tie sufficiently, the item will not fall off. If you're using a wheel and the item is very large, you may need to stop and coax it through the orifice and flyer hooks onto the bobbin.

For small dashes of color, add bits of purchased fibers such as shredded sari silk, Angelina (a glittery microfiber that is soft to the touch), or even snippets of yarn. You may find that you have deposited a nice collection of fiber pieces on the floor next to you—chunks that got tangled and were too bothersome to deal with as your were spinning, fluffy bits that fell off of your well-prepared roving, etc. Don't throw these out. Save them, fluff them up, and spin them into a one-of-a-kind yarn, either by themselves or with other fiber. You'll have fun seeing your scraps turn into an amazing yarn.

Ultimately, you have control over what you include in your yarn. As with any yarn choice, let your own good taste guide you.

Chapter 7

What to Do with All That Yarn

It doesn't matter if you've spun 25 yards or 2,500, there's something you can do with almost any amount of handspun. The patterns here will show you how to knit all-handspun items, and also how to combine handspun successfully with commercial yarn, maximizing the effect of your hard work and allowing you to begin knitting that much sooner. I'll show you how particular stitch patterns can even out uneven or biased yarn, and how to use gauge swatches instead of yarn labels to determine whether a pattern is right for the yarn you've spun.

Handspun yarn is not like commercial yarn. Repeat this to yourself a few more times. Okay, now say it again. You will need to throw out your assumptions (and many of your old habits) when it comes to such things as the lowly gauge swatch, as well as how a particular knitting style or tension affects the outcome of a pattern.

I admit I am not particularly scientific about either my spinning or knitting. Spinner June Oshiro of cabled DNA scarf fame (see the Fall 2003 issue of *Interweave Knits*) is my polar opposite—she can tell you at what angle her yarn was spun, the number of twists per inch, and just about anything else you'd like to know. Her yarns need their own trading cards, just to keep track of the stats. Not mine. Yet we both manage to get good results. So relax, it'll be okay no matter what your style. If you do want to learn more about grist, twist, and all the other technical measurements of yarn, I suggest reading *The Alden Amos Big Book of Handspinning* (Interweave Press, 2001).

The patterns in this book have considerable wiggle room. If your felted purse is an inch larger on one side than mine, where's the harm? The instructions for projects that must fit, such as the Faux Fair Isle Raglans on page 62, are written for the specific handspun yarn used—your own handspun and gauge are likely to be different.

Yarn Weight

Since you won't have a label to identify the weight of yarn you've produced or to suggest an appropriate needle size, you'll need to rely on a few numeric guidelines. In her book *Homespun, Hand-knit* (Interweave Press, 1987), Linda Ligon devised a useful chart (reproduced below) that, as a spinner, I find especially helpful.

More recently, the Craft Yarn Council of America (CYCA) introduced a standard yarn weight system, which is gradually being adopted by yarn manufacturers. According to CYCA, fingering, sport, DK, worsted, chunky, and bulky yarns are classified as "super fine, fine, light, medium, bulky, and super bulky." Whatever you call them, CYCA's recommended needle sizes for these yarns are slightly different from those shown below. Remember that these are only guidelines—especially when it comes to needle sizes.

You now have two ways to control the gauge of your knitted fabric—through your personal knitting style and tension and through the yarn you spin. But controlling the knitted fabric that results is another matter entirely, especially if you want to use handspun yarn in a pattern designed for commercial yarn. If your handspun isn't perfectly plied, for example, the knitted fabric may bias to one side or another and affect the look of the finished piece. This isn't a problem in some patterns, such as the top-down raglan Eddie Sweater on page 6, but a sweater knitted in pieces would be difficult to seam together if each piece tended to bias. How can you control the tendency of the fabric to slant without

SOME APPROXIMATIONS OF PLAIN YARNS				
Yarn Weight	Yards/Pound	WPI	Gauge in Stitches/Inch	U.S. Needle Size
Lace	2600+	18+	8+	00–2
Fingering	1900–2400	16	6–8	2–4
Sport	1200–1800	14	5–6.5	4–6
Worsted	900–1200	12	4–5	7–9
Bulky	600–800	10	3–4	10–11
Very bulky	400–500	8 or fewer	2–3	13–15

A very rough meters/kilogram measurement can be obtained by multiplying the yards/pound value by 2.

throwing out the yarn and spinning it all again? The answer is in stitch patterns.

Stitch Patterns

Stitch patterns affect yarn in a number of ways. You may already know that if you want to plug a stitch pattern into a garment designed for a different stitch pattern, you might need to adjust your gauge and the amount of yarn needed. For example, it takes more yarn to knit a row of seed stitch than plain stockinette stitch. Why? Because the process of moving the yarn from front to back and vice versa between the alternating knit and purl stitches creates small sideways floats of yarn between each stitch. The "sideways floats" in patterns such as seed stitch don't just affect the amount of yarn needed to knit a given row; they also help balance out overtwisted or otherwise imperfect yarn. You can use the structure of many different stitches to your advantage when "evening out" handspun yarn.

As a rule of thumb, balanced stitch patterns are best if your yarn is overtwisted or tends to bias to one side in stockinette stitch, assuming, of course, that you want to counteract the bias. (If you're knitting energized singles straight off the bobbin for the effect they give, you won't want to "correct" them in this way.) By "balanced" I mean that the stitch patterns employ equal numbers of knit and purl stitches both horizontally and vertically. Seed stitch, moss stitch, double moss stitch, and similar combinations are the most obvious choices. Use seed stitch if your yarn is extremely overtwisted. If it's a little less so, try a k2, p2 rib (line up columns of two knit stitches and columns of two

purl stitches). Experiment—the weight of yarn will also make a difference, so there's no one-size-fits-all solution. This is another reason to knit gauge swatches and try out different pattern stitches until you find the fabric you want.

With that, please allow me to reintroduce you to an old friend you may not have knitted in a while: the Humble Garter Stitch Scarf.

Garter stitch is an excellent choice when your yarn is a little "off" and you don't want to use a pattern stitch. It evens out odd thick/thin spots in otherwise regular yarn, too. If you've spun your very first yarn and want to get started on a project that is guaranteed to accommodate its quirks, knit a garter stitch scarf.

Overtwisted yarn tends to bias to one side when knitted in stockinette stitch.

The garter scarf gets a bad rap as a "beginners only" project; a boring, mindless bit of knitting that could be done in the dark. But it doesn't have to be that way, especially if you use your wonderful new handspun! The scarves pictured on pages 60 and 61 were knitted sideways, that is, from long edge to long edge instead of from short edge to short edge. This means that there are more stitches on the needle but fewer rows to knit. Just cast on 200–300 stitches, depending on the weight of your yarn and the length you want your scarf, then knit every stitch of every row until the scarf is the width you want, and bind off all of the stitches. When using handspun, it is much easier to hide slight differences in yarn weight that can distort the edges if the scarf is knitted along the wide dimension from side to side instead of along the narrow dimension from top to bottom.

This distortion, by the way, can be exaggerated as a design feature if you like the way it looks. Spin a yarn that varies wildly in weight from one yard to the next (whether intentionally or not), and knit a 4–6 inch (10–15 cm) wide garter scarf. The edge will ripple irregularly on either side. Pick up the edges on a long circular needle and knit or crochet an edging in a contrasting color to highlight the effect.

Check out the following two garter stitch scarves. The scarf on page 60 began as several Fleece Artist rovings. I spun the rovings into singles, one roving at a time, then immediately knitted the singles sideways in garter stitch until I had used up all the yarn. The singles was overtwisted, yet no fabric bias is obvious in the body of the scarf. The ends did curl slightly to one side, which was easily corrected with blocking.

The scarf on page 61 uses black Crystal Palace Shag, Malabrigo, and a super-multicolor yarn by Lexi Boeger of Pluckyfluff in the center. The Malabrigo yarn was cast on provisionally and knitted for several rows before changing to the Pluckyfluff and back again to Malabrigo. I often cast on provisionally for these types of scarves because it makes it easier to add other colors or edging after the fact. In this case, I thought the scarf needed a little "oomph," so I added the soft Shag, held double, to create a textured edge.

If you cast on provisionally every time, you can make a "sampler" scarf with a row of each yarn you spin, choosing the edging and/or fringe after the fact. It's the knitting equivalent of a patchwork quilt made from memorable fabrics—your first yarn, the yarn you spun from a friend's sheep, a handspun yarn you bought on vacation, etc.

Garter Scarf 1

Finished Size About 4½" (11.5 cm) wide and 46" (117 cm) long.

Yarn CYCA #4 Medium (worsted-weight) yarn: about 5½ oz (155 g). *Shown here:* Handspun singles from three different Fleece Artist rovings spun by Shannon Okey.

Needles Size 8 (5 mm): 32" (80 cm) circular (cir).

Notions Tapestry needle.

Gauge About 17½ sts and 36 rows = 4" (10 cm) in garter stitch. Your handspun yarn and gauge may vary.

Scarf

CO 200 sts. Changing colors every 2 rows, work 40 rows in garter st. BO all sts.

Finishing

Weave in loose ends. Block lightly.

Garter Scarf 2

Finished Size About 4½" (11.5 cm) wide and 86"
(218.5 cm) long.

Yarn CYCA #4 Medium (worsted-weight) yarn:
about 215 yd (196 m) color A, about 90 yd
[82 m] color B, and about 57 yd [52 m] color
C. *Shown here:* Malabrigo Worsted Merino
(100% merino; 215 yd [196 m]/100 g): cypress
(green, A), 1 skein. Multicolored handspun yarn
by Lexi Boeger of Pluckyfluff (wool, Angelina,
and other fiber scraps; about 12 wraps per
inch [2.5 cm]): multicolored (B), 90 yd (82 m).
Crystal Palace Shag (45% wool, 45% acrylic,
10% nylon eyelash; 57 yd [52 m]/50 g): #0202
ebony (C), 1 ball.

Needles Size 8 (5 mm): 32" (80 cm) circular.

Notions Smooth waste yarn for provisional cast-
on; tapestry needle.

Gauge About 15 sts and 32 rows = 4" (10 cm) in
garter st with Malabrigo. Your handspun yarn
and gauge may vary.

Note

The fiber "puffs" visible on the scarf shown are part
of handspun yarn B.

Scarf

With A and using the provisional method (see
Glossary, page 122), CO 320 sts. Work 9 rows even
in garter st. Change to B and work even in garter st
for 14 rows. Change to A and work even in garter st
for 9 more rows. With 2 strands of C held together,
knit 2 rows. BO all sts. Carefully remove waste
yarn from provisional CO and place exposed sts on
needle. With 2 strands of C held tog, knit 2 rows.
BO all sts.

Finishing

Weave in loose ends. Block lightly.

Faux Fair Isle Raglans

Shannon Okey and Symeon North

This pattern is infinitely adjustable to suit a wide range of sizes and yarns. If you wanted, you could probably swap yarns every other row for a stash-busting striped sweater extraordinaire. Hong Kong Garden (page 62), the teal version made with Noro plus handspun from Morehouse Merino fleece, is named after a Siouxsie and the Banshees song. Yes, I know Noro isn't from Hong Kong, but the name stuck. Handspun yarn by Symeon North (see her Pippi Socks on page 69) plus Cascade Eco Wool went into Forsythia (page 66), the yellow and brown version. I asked Symeon to dye the handspun to look like a forsythia bush in early spring—yellow blossoms bursting out of a "woody" brown section.

Hong Kong Garden
(teal and white version)

Yoke

With medium-length cir needle and CC (shown here: CC1), CO 100 sts. Place marker (pm) and join for working in the rnd, being careful not to twist sts. Work seed st as foll:

Rnd 1: *K1, p1; rep from * to end of rnd.
Rnd 2: *P1, k1; rep from * to end of rnd.
Rep these 2 rnds 4 more times—10 rnds total. *Next*

Finished Size Can be customized for adult finished chest 36" (91.5 cm) to 52" (132 cm). Shown in size 50" (127 cm).

Yarn CYCA #4 Medium (worsted-weight) yarn, for finished chest sizes 36 (44, 52)" (91.5 [112, 132] cm): about 1200 (1500, 2000) yd (1097 [1371, 1829] m), divided as desired between main color (MC) for body and sleeves and contrast color (CC) for yoke. *Shown here:* Handspun yarn (100% merino wool from Morehouse Merinos fleece, carded into roving by Wooly Knob) in natural (MC), spun as a slightly overtwisted singles in approximately worsted-weight by Shannon Okey. Noro Silk Garden (45% silk, 45% kid mohair, 10% lambswool; 109 yd [100 m]/ 50 g): #208 turquoise, teal, gray mix (CC1). Noro Kureyon (100% wool; 109 yd [100 m]/ 50 g): #150 green and gray mix (CC2).

Needles Size 8 (5 mm): 16", 24", and 32" (40, 60, and 80 cm) circular (cir).

Notions Markers (m); waste yarn or stitch holders; tapestry needle.

Gauge 16½–18 sts and 25–31 rnds = 4" (10 cm) in St st worked in the rnd. For the sweater shown, 18 sts and 31 rnds = 4" (10 cm) in St st using MC, and 16½ sts and 25 rnds = 4" (10 cm) in St st using CC. Your handspun yarn and gauge may vary.

rnd: K15 for right sleeve, pm, k35 for front, pm, k15 for left sleeve, pm, k35 for back—35 sts each for front and back, 15 sts for each sleeve; rnd begins at back right raglan line. *Inc rnd:* *K1f&b (see Glossary, page 123), knit to next m, k1f&b, slip marker (sl m); rep from * 3 more times—8 sts inc'd, 1 st on each side of all 4 markers. Knit 1 rnd even. Rep the last 2 rnds until sweater reaches to your underarms, changing to longest cir needle if necessary, and periodically slipping the sts onto a length of waste yarn to try on the sweater and check your progress. *Note:* For the sweater shown, CC1 was used until the ball ran out, then CC2 was used until that ball ran out, then MC was used; the yoke shown measures about 9½" (24 cm) from end of seed st neckband to beg of armholes.

Body

Place the sleeve sts in the two smaller marked sections on lengths of waste yarn or stitch holders. If you have not already done so, change to MC and join yarn to beg of front sts with RS facing. Calculate the number of sts needed to CO at each armhole gap (see Tip on page 67). Knit across the front sts to the gap from left sleeve, use the backward loop method (see Glossary, page 121) to CO the desired number of sts for the left armhole, knit across the back sts to the next gap, use the backward loop method to CO the desired number of sts for the right armhole, pm, and join for working in the rnd. Cont in St st in the rnd until the body is the desired length, including your choice of edging. Loosely BO all sts. *Note:* For the sweater shown, St st was worked until the body measured 11" (28 cm) from armholes, then seed st was worked for 1" (2.5 cm).

Sleeves

Place held sts for one sleeve on shortest cir needle and rejoin MC with RS facing to beg of sts CO for armhole gap. Pick up and knit 1 st for each CO st at armhole, placing m at the center of these sts to indicate end of rnd aligned with center of underarm, knit across sleeve sts, then knit the first half of picked-up sts again to end at the marker. Work even in St st for about 1" (2.5 cm). *Dec rnd:* K2tog, knit to last 2 sts, k2tog tbl (see Glossary, page 122)—2 sts dec'd. *Note:* If you prefer, you may substitute an ssk decrease (see Glossary, page 122), which is also a left-leaning decrease, for k2tog tbl at the end of the dec rnd. Work even in St st until piece measures 1" (2.5 cm) from beg of dec rnd, and note how many rnds total you have worked from beg of dec rnd. Rep the last 1" (2.5 cm) of rnds (dec rnd followed by rnds worked even) until sleeve measures desired finished length minus any edging, or until sleeve cuff has reached the desired circumference. If necessary, cont even in St st after reaching cuff circumference until sleeve measures desired length, minus any edging. For a rolled cuff, work about 1–2" (2.5–5 cm) longer to allow the cuff to roll. If not making a rolled cuff, work edging of your choice. Loosely BO all sts. *Note:* For the sweater shown, St st was worked until sleeve measured 11" (28 cm) from armhole, then seed st was worked for 1" (2.5 cm) for a wide, short sleeve. Make second sleeve the same as the first.

Finishing

Weave in loose ends. Block lightly to desired measurements.

Forsythia
(yellow and brown version)

Yoke

With shorter-length smaller cir needle and MC, CO 76 sts. Place marker (pm) and join for working in the rnd, being careful not to twist sts. Work in k1, p1 rib for 1¼" (3.2 cm). Change to CC and shorter-length larger cir needle. *Next rnd:* K15 for right sleeve, pm, k23 for front, pm, k15 for left sleeve, pm, k23 for back—23 sts each for front and back, 15 sts for each sleeve; rnd begins at back right raglan line. Work even in St st until piece measures 1" (2.5 cm) from last rnd of k1, p1 rib. *Inc rnd:* *K1f&b (see Glossary, page 123), knit to next m, k1f&b, slip marker (sl m); rep from * 3 more times—8 sts inc'd, 1 st on each side of all 4 markers. Knit 1 rnd even. Rep the last 2 rnds until sweater reaches to your underarms, changing to longer-length larger cir needle if necessary and periodically slipping the sts onto a length of waste yarn to try on the sweater and check your progress. *Note:* For the sweater shown, CC was used until the ball ran out, then MC was used along with smaller cir needle; the yoke shown measures about 8¾" (22 cm) from end of ribbed neckband to beg of armholes.

Body

Place the sleeve sts in the two smaller marked sections on lengths of waste yarn or stitch holders. If you have not already done so, change to MC and longer-length smaller cir needle, and rejoin MC to beg of front sts with RS facing. Calculate the number

Finished Size Can be customized for adult finished chest 36" (91.5 cm) to 52" (132 cm). Shown in size 40" (101.5 cm).

Yarn CYCA #4 Medium (worsted-weight) yarn, for finished chest sizes 36 (44, 52)" (91.5 [112, 132] cm): about 900 (1125, 1500) yd (823 [1029, 1372] m) in main color (MC) for body and sleeves. CYCA #5 Bulky (chunky-weight) yarn: about 250 (300, 400) yd (229 [274, 366] m) in contrast color (CC) for yoke. *Shown here:* Cascade Yarns Eco-Wool (100% wool; 478 yd [437 m]/250 g): #8025 natural dark brown (MC), 2 skeins. Handspun thick and thin yarn (100% wool; ranging from 3–6 wraps per inch): forsythia yellow (CC) hand-dyed with cake frosting dyes by Symeon North.

Needles Size 11 (8 mm): 16" and 24" (40 and 60 cm) circular (cir). Size 13 (9 mm): 24" and 32" (60 and 80 cm) cir.

Notions Markers (m); waste yarn or stitch holders; tapestry needle.

Gauge 11½–14 sts and 16–18 rnds = 4" (10 cm) in St st worked in the rnd using MC and smaller needle; 10–12 sts and 15–16 rnds = 4" (10 cm) using CC and larger needle. For the sweater shown, 11½ sts and 18 rnds = 4" (10 cm) in St st using MC and smaller needle; 10 sts and 15 rnds = 4" (10 cm) in St st using CC and larger needle. Your handspun yarn and gauge may vary.

of sts needed to CO at each armhole gap (see Tip below). Knit across the front sts to the gap from left sleeve, use the backward loop method (see Glossary, page 121) to CO the desired number of sts for the left armhole, knit across the back sts to the next gap, use the backward loop method to CO the desired number of sts for the right armhole, pm, and join for working in the rnd. Cont in St st in the rnd until the body is 2½" to 3" (6.5 to 7.5 cm) less than desired finished length, adjusting the st count to be a multiple of 4 sts in the last rnd. Work in k2, p2 rib for 2½" (6.5 cm). Loosely BO all sts in rib patt. *Note:* For the sweater shown, St st was worked until the body measured 11" (28 cm) from armholes, then k2, p2 rib was worked for 3" (7.5 cm).

Sleeves

Place held sts for one sleeve on shorter-length smaller cir needle and rejoin MC with RS facing to beg of sts CO for armhole gap. Pick up and knit 1 st for each CO st at armhole, placing m at the center of these sts to indicate end of rnd aligned with center of underarm, knit across sleeve sts, then knit the first half of picked-up sts again to end at m. Work even in St st for about 1" (2.5 cm). *Dec rnd:* K2tog, knit to last 2 sts, k2tog tbl (see Glossary, page 122)—2 sts dec'd. *Note:* If you prefer, you may substitute an ssk decrease (see Glossary, page 122), which is also a left-leaning decrease, for k2tog tbl at the end of the dec rnd. Work even in St st until piece measures 1"

(2.5 cm) from beg of dec rnd, and note how many rnds total you have worked from beg of dec rnd. Rep the last 1" (2.5 cm) of rnds (dec rnd followed by rnds worked even) until sleeve measures 2½" (6.5 cm) less than desired finished length, or sleeve cuff has reached the desired circumference, adjusting the st count to be a multiple of 4 sts in the last rnd. If necessary, cont even in St st after reaching cuff circumference until sleeve measures 2½" (6.5 cm) less than desired finished length. Work in k2, p2 rib for 2½" (6.5 cm). Loosely BO all sts in rib patt. *Note:* For the sweater shown, St st was worked until the sleeve measured 18" (45.5 cm) from armhole, then k2, p2 rib was worked for 2½" (6.5 cm). Make second sleeve the same as the first.

Finishing

Weave in loose ends. Block lightly to desired measurements.

TIP
The number of stitches to cast on for each underarm gap should equal about one-fourth of the sleeve stitches at the dividing round. If your body yarn is thinner than your yoke yarn, you may need to cast on more than one-fourth the sleeve stitches; if your body yarn is thicker than your yoke yarn, you may need to cast on fewer stitches.

Symeon North

Symeon North likes to call herself a "Vermont-based domestic revolutionary and mother of two." Add "dyepot genius" to the list and you're edging closer to a full and accurate description. Symeon has a long history of textile work. Before settling in Vermont, she traveled around the country, supporting herself by selling handmade clothes and other fabric accessories. Symeon brings these varied experiences to her art in unexpectedly beautiful color combinations and yarn styles. Her thick/thin yarn (as seen in the Faux Fair Isle Sweater on page 66) makes even plain stockinette stitch look special—up close, the yarn looks like a heavily textured specialty yarn.

Symeon's husband recently built her an electric spinner out of an old sewing machine motor and a used flyer assembly. Although this has allowed her to increase her production and spinning speed without resorting to outside help, Symeon still loves spinning on her older traditional wheel. Her business, Pippi Knee Socks, has been booming ever since knitters discovered her unique yarn a few years ago. Her Pippi Socks on page 69 are dense, soft, and comfortable—perfect for a winter's day, inside or out. When you live within walking distance of both the Ben & Jerry's factory and ski resorts—like Symeon does—it's good to have a nice thick pair of socks to keep your feet warm!

Visit Symeon's website at www.pippikneesocks.com

Pippi Socks

Symeon North

These socks were made from the very first yarn spun on Symeon's homemade electric spinner. The yarn was spun from Falklands wool at a high number of twists per inch, then plied on her Ashford Traditional wheel. The yarn came in at a lovely 12 wraps per inch and took roughly 250 yards to knit these socks on size 5 needles. For once in her entire sock-making history, Symeon didn't suffer from the dreaded Second Sock Syndrome. (You've probably had this yourself, if you knit socks—you finish one and then it sits, alone and unloved, waiting for you to finish its mate.)

Finished Size About 8" (20.5 cm) foot circumference and 9½" (24 cm) long from back of heel to tip of toe; to fit woman's U.S. shoe sizes 8 to 9.

Yarn CYCA #4 Medium (worsted-weight) yarn: about 250–300 yd (229–274 m).
Shown here: Handspun, hand-dyed 100% wool yarn by Symeon North.

Needles Size 5 (3.75 mm): set of 4 double-pointed (dpn) or one or two long circular (cir). See Note on page 70.

Notions Marker (m); stitch holder or waste yarn; tapestry needle.

Gauge About 11 sts and 18 rnds = 2" (5 cm) in St st worked in the rnd; this gauge is deliberately tighter than usual for worsted-weight yarn. Your handspun and gauge may vary.

Note

Some people prefer to use circular needles to knit socks; others prefer double-pointed needles. This pattern is written without any specific references to Needle 1, Needle 2, etc., and therefore does not favor one type of needle over the other. To work these socks on double-pointed needles, divide the total stitches onto three needles—11 stitches on each of two needles (for the back half of the leg or the heel and sole) and 22 stitches on a third needle (for the front half of the leg or the instep). To knit these socks on one or two long circular needles, divide the stitches into two groups of 22 stitches each—one group for the back of leg, heel, and sole; the other for the front of leg and instep. For both methods, after working the heel flap, arrange the stitches so that the end of the round is in the center of the heel stitches.

Leg

CO 44 sts. Place marker (pm) and join for working in the rnd, being careful not to twist sts. Work k1, p1 rib for 22 rnds—piece measures about 2½" (6.5 cm) from CO. Change to St st (knit every rnd) and work even until piece measures about 8" (20.5 cm) from CO.

Heel

Heel Flap

Place last 22 sts of previous rnd on holder or length of waste yarn for instep. Work 22 heel sts back and forth in rows as foll:

Row 1: (RS) Sl 1, *k1, sl 1 pwise with yarn in back; rep from * to last st, k1.

Row 2: Sl 1, purl to end.

Rep Rows 1 and 2 until a total of 24 rows have been worked for the heel flap, ending with Row 2.

Turn Heel

Work short-rows (see Glossary, page 125) as foll:

Row 1: (RS) K12, ssk, k1, turn work.
Row 2: Sl 1, p3, p2tog, p1, turn.
Row 3: Sl 1, k4, ssk, k1, turn.
Row 4: Sl 1, p5, p2tog, p1, turn.
Row 5: Sl 1, k6, ssk, k1, turn.
Row 6: Sl 1, p7, p2tog, p1, turn.
Row 7: Sl 1, k8, ssk, k1, turn.
Row 8: Sl 1, p9, p2tog, p1, turn.
Row 9: Sl 1, k10, ssk, turn.
Row 10: Sl 1, p10, p2tog—12 heel sts rem.

Gussets

Rejoin for working in the rnd as foll:

Rnd 1: With RS facing, k12 heel sts, pick up and knit 12 sts from slipped selvedge sts along side of heel flap, pick up and knit 1 st through the back loop (tbl) between heel flap and instep sts to prevent a hole, k22 instep sts, pick up and knit 1 st tbl between instep sts and heel flap, pick up and knit 12 sts from slipped sts along other side of heel flap, knit first 6 heel sts again—60 sts total; rnd begins at center of heel sts.

Rnd 2: Knit to last 3 heel sts, k2tog, k1, k22 instep sts, k1, ssk, knit to end—2 sts dec'd.

Rnd 3: Knit.

Rep Rnds 2 and 3 seven more times—44 sts rem.

Foot

Work even in St st until piece measures about 7¾"
(19.5 cm) from back of heel, or about 1¾" (4.5 cm)
less than desired total length.

Toe

Dec for toe as foll:

Rnd 1: K8, k2tog, k2, ssk, k16, k2tog, k2, ssk,
k8—40 sts rem.

Rnd 2 and all even-numbered rnds: Knit.

Rnd 3: K7, k2tog, k2, ssk, k14, k2tog, k2, ssk,
k7—36 sts rem.

Rnd 5: K6, k2tog, k2, ssk, k12, k2tog, k2, ssk,
k6—32 sts rem.

Rnd 7: K5, k2tog, k2, ssk, k10, k2tog, k2, ssk,
k5—28 sts rem.

Rnd 9: K4, k2tog, k2, ssk, k8, k2tog, k2, ssk, k4—24
sts rem.

Rnd 11: K3, k2tog, k2, ssk, k6, k2tog, k2, ssk,
k3—20 sts rem.

Rnd 13: K2, k2tog, k2, ssk, k4, k2tog, k2, ssk,
k2—16 sts rem.

Finishing

Work first 4 sts of round again. Divide sts evenly
between 2 needles so that 8 instep sts are on one
needle and 8 sole sts are on the other. Cut yarn,
leaving a 12" (30.5 cm) tail. Thread tail on a tapestry needle and use the Kitchener st (see Glossary,
page 125) to graft the sts tog. Weave in loose
ends. Block lightly.

Angela Ho

Angela Ho attracts spinning wheels
like magnets attract iron, and she has
quite a collection in her Vancouver
home—as well as a stash of gorgeous fibers.
She likes to knit lacy, light fabrics with her
handspun. But what's unique about Angela is
her creative bent for solving spinning problems.

Angela came up with a fun technique for
spinning multiple-ply yarns. To keep the plies
aligned as she's plying, Angela threads each ply
through a different hole in the cap from a spice
shaker—her own homemade plying template.
Hold the spice cap behind your fiber-feeding
hand and support and guide the plies onto
the bobbin with your nondominant hand.

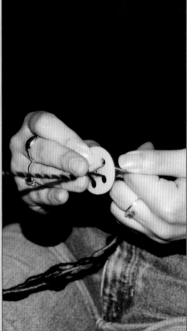

Pythagoras Ski Headband

Shannon Okey

Why Pythagoras? I was thinking about the diagonal angles I wanted in this headband and couldn't for the life of me remember which theorem it was that I needed (a mathematician I am not). So when I finally determined that maybe Pythagoras could be of assistance, I decided to name it after him, too. This is a great way to use up tiny bits of handspun. All the yarns here are from Houndscroft Farm. They include not only wool but also alpaca, cotton, sari silk, Angelina, and tiny beads.

Note

Use yarns at random, changing every 2 to 8 rows as desired, or until a yarn runs out.

Headband

CO 11 sts.

Row 1: K1, k8 wrapping the yarn twice around the needle for each st, k2.

Row 2: K2tog tbl (see Glossary, page 122), k8 dropping extra wraps as you come to them, k1f&b (see Glossary, page 123).

Rep Rows 1 and 2 until piece measures 21" (53.5 cm) from CO, measured along a selvedge. BO all sts.

Finishing

With yarn threaded on a tapestry needle, sew CO edge to BO edge. Weave in loose ends.

Pillbox Hat Variation

To make this into a pillbox-style hat, you will need a 16" (40 cm) circular needle (cir), a set of 4 or 5 double pointed needles (dpn), stitch marker (m), and additional yarn. With cir needle and RS of headband facing, pick up and knit about 2 sts for each garter ridge along one selvedge, making sure you have a multiple of 4 sts. Place marker (pm) and join for working in the rnd. Purl 1 rnd for garter st worked in the rnd. *Dec rnd:* K2tog, k2; rep from * to end of rnd. *Next rnd:* Purl 1 rnd. Cont in this manner, dec 1 out of every 4 sts as evenly as possible each knit dec rnd (fudge the last few sts of the rnd if you have to), then work 1 purl rnd even, until 8–12 sts rem or you have reached the center of the crown. Cut yarn, leaving a 10" (25.5 cm) tail. Thread tail on tapestry needle, draw through rem sts, pull tight to close top, and fasten off on WS. Weave in loose ends.

Finished Size About 3½" (9 cm) wide and 21" (53.5 cm) head circumference with fabric relaxed; will stretch to fit up to 24" (61 cm).

Yarn CYCA #4 Medium (worsted-weight) yarn: about 80 yd (70 m) total in several natural colors and fiber blends. *Shown here:* Handspun yarn by Houndscroft Farm: Centaur (wool, Angelina; about 4.5–5 wraps per inch): 8 yd (7 m); Darjeeling (wool, sari silk; about 3.5 wraps per inch): 6 yd (5.5 m); Zebra (alpaca, Icelandic wool; about 4 wraps per inch): 40 yd (37 m); Lion's Tail (wool, alpaca; about 3 wraps per inch): 11 yd (10 m); Wood Elf (wool, cotton, alpaca, beads; about 4.5–5 wraps per inch): 15 yd (10 m).

Needles Size 10½ (6.5 mm): straight.

Notions Tapestry needle.

Gauge 6½ sts and 9 rows = 4" (10 cm) in elongated diagonal garter stitch pattern. Exact gauge is not critical for this project. Your handspun yarn and gauge may vary.

Laurabelle Swedish Heart Shrug

Shannon Okey

Kristen Welsh spun the mauve-pink handspun used in the Swedish Heart Shrug. Her spinning notes are included on pages 78–79 to give you an idea of her thought process and the techniques she used to determine her perfect yarn from one roving. If entrelac knitting creates a faux basketweave effect, what we have here is faux entrelac, or the real thing—actual basketweave created by weaving narrow knitted strips for the diamond-shaped back panel and cuffs.

Notes

- Each sleeve begins with a provisional cast-on at center back and is worked outward to the edge of the body. Then new stitches are cast on for the front of the sleeve and the stitches are joined for working in the round downward to the cuff. Individual sawtooth points worked along the cuff edge provide a foundation for the basketwoven strips of the trim.
- After the sleeves have been joined and front edging is completed, there will be an upside-down V-shaped opening in the center of the back. The stitches for the back panel strips are picked up along both sides of this V, knitted to the required length, then interwoven as for the cuff trim to form the center back panel.

Left Sleeve

Using the provisional method (see Glossary, page 122) and longer cir needle, CO 10 sts. With MC, work in St st, inc at lower back edge (end of RS rows, beg of WS rows) as foll:

Finished Size 56 (60, 66)" (142 [152.5, 167.5] cm) long from cuff to cuff, and 17½" (44.5 cm) long from upper edge of back neck ribbing to bottom of center back point.

Yarn CYCA #4 Medium (worsted-weight) yarn: about 800 (850, 900) yd (732 [777, 823] m) commercial yarn for main color (MC), and 170 yd (155 m) handspun yarn for contrast color (CC).
Shown here: Brown Sheep Lamb's Pride Worsted (85% wool, 15% mohair; 190 yd [174 m]/4 oz [114] g): #M03 grey heather (MC), 5 skeins for all sizes. Handspun yarn from Winderwood Farm's hand-dyed roving (100% Corriedale 2-ply wool; about 10–12 wraps per inch): rose/orange mix (CC), 170 yd (155 m).

Needles Size 10½ (6.5 mm): 16" and 24" (40 and 60 cm) circular (cir).

Notions Waste yarn for provisional cast-on; markers (m); stitch holders; tapestry needle; safety pins; sewing thread and sharp-point sewing needle for finishing.

Gauge 15 sts and 21 rows = 4" (10 cm) in St st using MC. Your handspun yarn and gauge may vary.

Row 1: (RS) Knit to last 2 sts, k1f&b (see Glossary, page 123), k1—1 st inc'd.

Row 2: (WS) P1, p1f&b (see Glossary, page 124), purl to end—1 st inc'd.

Row 3: Knit.

Row 4: Rep Row 2—1 st inc'd.

Row 5: Rep Row 1—1 st inc'd.

Row 6: Purl

Rep Rows 1–6 four more times—30 sts; piece measures about 5¾" (14.5 cm) from CO. Cont inc's at lower back edge, and *at the same time* shape back neck edge (beg of RS rows; end of WS rows) as foll:

Row 1: (RS) K1, k1f&b, knit to last 2 sts, k1f&b, k1—2 sts inc'd.

Row 2: (WS) P1, p1f&b, purl to last 2 sts, p1f&b, p1—2 sts inc'd.

Rows 3, 5, 7, 9, and 11: K1, k1f&b, knit to end—1 st inc'd.

Rows 4, 6, 8, and 10: Rep Row 2.

Row 12: P1, p1f&b, purl to end—48 sts; piece measures about 8" (20.5 cm) from CO.

With RS facing, k48, place marker (pm) to indicate beg of sleeve rnd at underarm, use a provisional method to CO 47 sts onto left needle, knit across new sts, then knit first 48 sts again to end at end-of-rnd m—95 sts total; rnd begs at start of new sts. Work 3 rnds even in St st. *Dec rnd:* K2tog, knit to last 2 sts, k2tog tbl (see Glossary, page 122)—2 sts dec'd. *Note:* If you prefer, you may substitute an ssk decrease (see Glossary, page 122), which is also a left-leaning decrease, for k2tog tbl at the end of the dec rnd. Work 3 (4, 5) rnds even. Rep the last 4 (5, 6) rnds 15 more times, changing to shorter cir needle if necessary—63 sts rem for all sizes; sleeve measures about 12¾ (15¾, 19)" (32.5 [40, 48.5] cm) from beg of working in the rnd. Work even in St st until sleeve measures 14½ (16½, 19½)" (37 [42, 49.5] cm) from beg of working in the rnd, or about 5½" (14 cm) less than desired total length.

Triangles

Work first 9 sts back and forth in rows to form a triangle as foll:

Row 1: (RS) K9, turn.

Row 2: (WS) P9, turn.

Row 3: K2tog tbl, k5, k2tog, turn—7 sts in triangle.

Row 4: P7, turn.

Row 5: K2tog tbl, k3, k2tog, turn—5 sts in triangle.

Row 6: P5, turn.

Row 7: K2tog tbl, k1, k2tog, turn—3 sts in triangle.

Row 8: P3, turn.

Row 9: K2tog tbl, slip resulting st back to left needle, k2tog—1 st rem.

Cut yarn and draw through last st to fasten off. With RS facing, rejoin MC to next group of 9 sts, and work another triangle in the same manner. Work rem sleeve sts in 5 more triangles in the same way—7 triangles.

Strips

Hold sleeve with triangles pointing upwards. Join CC with RS facing to the top of one triangle point. With shorter cir needle, pick up and knit 9 sts from "peak" of triangle to bottom of "valley" between triangles. Work even in St st until strip measures 6" (15 cm) from pick-up row, ending with a WS row. Place sts on holder. Work 6 more 9-st strips using CC in the same manner. Join MC with RS facing to the bottom of the "valley" between two triangles. With shorter cir needle, pick up and knit 9 sts from "valley" between triangles to "peak" at top of triangle. Work even in St st until strip measures 6" (15 cm) from pick-up row, ending with a WS row.

Place sts on holder. Work 6 more 9-st strips using MC in the same manner.

Weave Strips

Note: Block the strips flat if they are curling so much that they resemble tubes rather than flat strips. Beg with a CC strip, *weave the strip over one MC strip, then under the next MC strip; rep from * once. Align live sts at end of CC strip with selvedge of MC strip and temporarily pin end of CC strip to the underside of MC strip. Weave the rem 6 CC strips in the same manner.

Rolled Cuff Edging

Return held sts to shorter cir needle, alternating 9 sts from a MC strip with 9 sts of a CC strip all the way around the cuff—126 sts total. If necessary, slip sts around needle without working them so the first sts to be worked will be the 9 sts of an MC strip aligned as nearly as possible above the sleeve dec line. Join MC with RS facing and pm for beg of rnd. Work even in St st for 4 rnds. Loosely BO all sts.

Right Sleeve

Using a provisional method and longer cir needle, CO 10 sts. With MC, work in St st, inc at lower back edge (beg of RS rows, end of WS rows) as foll:

Row 1: (RS) K1, k1f&b, knit to end—1 st inc'd.
Row 2: (WS) Purl to last 2 sts, p1f&b, p1—1 st inc'd.
Row 3: Knit.
Row 4: Rep Row 2—1 st inc'd.
Row 5: Rep Row 1—1 st inc'd.
Row 6: Purl

Rep Rows 1–6 four more times—30 sts; piece measures about 5¾" (14.5 cm) from CO. Cont inc's at lower back edge, and *at the same time* shape back neck edge (end of RS rows; beg of WS rows) as foll:

Row 1: (RS) K1, k1f&b, knit to last 2 sts, k1f&b, k1—2 sts inc'd.
Row 2: (WS) P1, p1f&b, purl to last 2 sts, p1f&b, p1—2 sts inc'd.
Rows 3, 5, 7, 9, and 11: Knit to last 2 sts, k1f&b, k1—1 st inc'd.
Rows 4, 6, 8, and 10: Rep Row 2.
Row 12: Purl to last 2 sts, p1f&b, p1—48 sts; piece measures about 8" (20.5 cm) from CO.

With RS facing, pm to indicate beg of sleeve rnd at underarm, k48, use a provisional method to CO 47 sts onto left needle, knit across new sts—95 sts total; rnd begs at start of original sleeve sts. Complete sleeve, triangles, strips, weave strips, and rolled cuff edging as for left sleeve.

Join Sleeves

Carefully remove waste yarn from provisional CO at beg of each sleeve, and place 10 live sts from each sleeve on separate needle. With MC, use the Kitchener st (see Glossary, page 125) or three-needle bind-off method (see Glossary, page 120) to join sleeve sts tog at center back.

Front Edging

Carefully remove waste yarn from provisional CO along front edge of right sleeve, place 47 sts on longer cir needle, and join MC with RS facing. Knit across sts of right sleeve, pick up and knit 30 sts

A Yarn Tale: Spinning Notes from Kristen Welsh

I acquired the roving for the contrast yarn in the Laurabelle Swedish Heart Shrug (see page 74) at a fiber swap held at a meeting of my spinning guild (Genesee Valley Handspinners Guild; www.gvhg.org). I had been spinning for just over three years when I got the roving, and while I have spun a good bit of variegated handpainted roving—including roving I've dyed myself—this particular roving presented some challenges. It had many more individual colors than any other I'd used, not all of the colors were in the same family (there were reds, pinks, browns, oranges, and blues), and each color repeat was fairly small. I was worried about how to keep the colors from combining into an extremely complex shade of mud. So, like many spinners, I set the roving aside to age.

When I decided that the roving would be the perfect project for this book, I pulled it out of my stash and thought again about how to handle it. I was afraid that if I just sat down to spin I'd have a disaster on my hands. Since the entire four ounces was one thick, unbroken length of roving, it seemed a safe bet to split the roving along its length and treat each length the same way. I made four strips, roughly one ounce each, and decided to use one full ounce for sampling and experimentation. I split that strip again into two sections, predrafted, and started to spin. The first decision I had to make was how thick I wanted the yarn to be. Using a short, forward draft, I drafted 2 inches (5 cm) of fiber but varied the number of treadles on my Journey Wheel that accompanied each drafted length in a technique I had learned just a few months earlier in a Rita Buchanan class, the only spinning class I've ever taken. I discovered that just

one treadle per drafted length gave a bouncy, lofty yarn, while additional treadles made a finer, almost wiry yarn. This was a surprise because I love to spin very fine yarns, but with this roving, the fluffier effect was the clear winner.

Next, I had to decide how to handle the colors. I knew that I didn't want to Navajo ply, because I wanted to get as much yardage as possible out of this small amount of roving and because I wanted to keep the spinning process as simple as possible for the book. I considered three other options: spinning each complete strip of roving and plying it back on itself; spinning each complete strip of roving onto two separate bobbins, then plying the singles from those two bobbins together; and carding one strip of roving with itself using handcards, then plying the yarn spun from the re-carded roving with a singles spun from the original roving, a technique I learned from a Patsy Zawistoski video in which she calls it "making the perfect neutral." I worried that the first option might have too much variety in the color changes, and knew from previous attempts that the second option—essentially an attempt to line up color repeats from two separate bobbins—was easier in theory than in practice. The third option seemed like the way to go. Still, I decided to sample each approach, using the rest of the one ounce of roving that I'd used to determine my drafting/treadling pattern.

When I had finished sampling, I was surprised to discover that the differences between the yarns made from the different techniques were less than I'd expected, but still noticeable. The "plied-on-itself" *yarn was definitely the wildest of the three, but not overwhelmingly so. The yarn made with one ply of the "perfect neutral" was the "quietest" of the three; from across the room, my eye perceived it as mauve yarn with occasional flecks of orange or blue—pretty, but not as lively as the other two yarns. The "middle" yarn, made from two parallel lengths of roving, had the coherence of the "perfect neutral" yarn and the life of the "plied-on-itself" yarn. It was, to quote Goldilocks, "just right."*

My technique was set, and I was off. I split each of my remaining one-ounce strips of roving along its length, then spun each half-ounce strip and plied it with its twin. I've rarely done this much sampling and experimentation, but I am so pleased with the resulting yarn that I may have learned a new lesson!

Upon close examination of the samples Kristen sent, and knowing how they'd be arranged in the shrug (in narrow, individual strips rather than in a wider piece of fabric), I chose to use all the yarns she'd spun, not just the "Goldilocks" yarn. The differences are subtle from afar but quite startling up close, and the neutral gray background yarn serves as the perfect backdrop for the colorful strips of handspun. Designing a pattern such as this *after* the yarn has been spun is often a challenge: if the yarn doesn't fit the look you're after, you may be out of luck. But it can be creative and fun, too. Try one of the smaller patterns (such as the Power Station Hat on page 89) with multiple yarns spun from the same roving in different ways to see how the knitted versions of the yarn compare with the singles straight off the bobbin. Often yarns will look very different once they are knitted.

along shaped neck edge of right sleeve to center back (about 3 sts for every 4 rows), pick up and knit 30 sts along shaped neck edge of left sleeve to beg of provisional CO sts, carefully remove waste yarn from provisional CO along front edge of left sleeve and place 47 sts on needle, and knit to end—154 sts total; do *not* join for working in the rnd. Working back and forth in rows, work in k1, p1 rib for 3 rows, ending with a WS row. *Next row:* (RS) [K2tog tbl] 2 times, knit to last 3 sts, k2tog, return last st worked to left needle, k2tog again—4 sts dec'd. Rep the last 4 rows 2 more times—142 sts rem; 12 rows k1, p1 rib completed; ribbing measures about 2" (5 cm) from pick-up row. BO all sts in patt.

Center Back Panel
Strips
Hold shrug with RS of back facing you, neck edge at bottom of work, and V-shaped opening at center back oriented like a V. Join MC with RS facing to bind-off row of front edging at top right corner of V (this is the lower left front when worn). With shorter cir needle, pick up and knit 50 sts from top corner of V to bottom of "valley" at base of V. Turn work. Work back and forth in St st on first 10 sts closest to the base of V until 10-st strip measures 11" (28 cm) from pick-up row, ending with a WS row. Place sts on holder. Work 4 more 10-st strips

TIP
If you use a nonwool yarn, carry some thin elastic in a matching color along with the MC for working the ribbing or use a blend containing elastic or lycra (such as Cascade Fixation) to help the shrug fit snugly around the bust and shoulders when worn.

using MC in the same manner. Join CC with RS facing to the bottom of the "valley" at base of V. With shorter cir needle, pick up and knit 50 sts from base of V to bind-off row of front edging at top left corner of V (this is the lower right front when worn). Turn work. Work back and forth in St st on first 10 sts closest to the top corner of V until 10-st strip measures 11" (28 cm) from pick-up row, ending with a WS row. Place sts on holder. Work 4 more 10-st strips using CC in the same manner.

Weave Strips

Note: Block the strips flat if they are curling so much that they resemble tubes rather than flat strips. Beg with the CC strip closest to the base of the V, *weave the strip over one MC strip, under the next MC strip; rep from * once more, then weave strip over last MC strip. Align live sts at end of CC strip with selvedge of MC strip and temporarily pin end of CC strip on top of MC strip. With the next CC strip out from the base of the V, *weave the strip under one MC strip, then over the next MC strip; rep from * once more, then weave strip under last MC strip. Align live sts at end of CC strip with selvedge of MC strip, and temporarily pin end of CC strip to underside of MC strip. Weave the rem 3 CC strips in the same manner, alternating whether each strip begins by going over or under an MC strip.

Lower Back Edging

Place 50 held CC strip sts in order on shorter cir needle and join CC with RS facing. BO all sts kwise. Place 50 held MC strip sts in order on shorter cir needle and join MC with RS facing. BO all sts kwise.

Finishing

Weave in all loose ends. Block to measurements. To prevent back panel edges from curling, use sewing thread and sharp-point needle to invisibly sew the unattached selvedges of the strips on each side of the center back point to the BO edge worked in the opposite color.

Holly Klump

Holly Klump, like so many other fiber artists, started off in another medium; in her case, it was paper arts. Her business, "misshawklet," offers handcrafted books and stationery with images "rescued" from yard sales and cancelled library books. Holly lives in Burlington, Vermont, a college town with many other knitters and spinners, near the New York/Canadian border where warm wool is a winter necessity.

Animal-friendliness is crucial to Holly, so she usually spins wool she obtains from Jim and Sandy Ryan at the Homestead in Monroe, Wisconsin, where abandoned or unwanted sheep are rescued to become pampered pets and fiber providers. Although sheep are not harmed when they are shorn (it's the equivalent of a human haircut), they are often sold for meat when they outlive their usefulness as breeding stock. Holly believes supporting farms such as the Homestead is one way to make a difference. See Resources on page 127 for other animal-friendly fiber providers.

Visit Holly's website at www.misshawklet.com

Betsey Bag

Shannon Okey

The Betsey in question is fashion designer Betsey Johnson, whom I always associate with flashy, fun clothing shapes and lots of color. This bag's side panels flare out like a tulle skirt, giving you a top that's easily closed *and* enough room at the bottom for all your stuff. Its messenger bag-style flap is knitted from handspun, hand-dyed yarn by Holly Klump, but it isn't felted. Using a simple provisional cast-on with nonfelting yarn, you can come back after the bag is felted to knit the flap. No sewing required!

Note
The bag body begins at the opening top edge and is worked downwards to the lower edge.

Stitch Guide
Seed Stitch (odd number of sts)
All Rows: *K1, p1; rep from * to last st, k1.

Broken Checkerboard Pattern (worked over 45 sts)
Set-up row: (WS) K5, p5, k10, [p5, k5] 2 times, p5.
Rows 1 and 3: (RS) [K5, p5] 2 times, k5, p10, k5, p5.
Rows 2 and 4: K5, p5, k10, [p5, k5] 2 times, p5.
Rows 5, 7, and 9: [P5, k5] 2 times, p20, k5.
Rows 6, 8, and 10: P5, k20, [p5, k5] 2 times.
Rows 11, 13, and 15: Rep Row 1.
Rows 12, 14, and 16: Rep Row 2.
Rows 17–40: Rep Row 5–16 two more times.

Bag Body
With MC, double strand of thick crochet cotton, and using the provisional method (see Glossary, page 122), CO 110 sts. Place marker (pm), and join

Finished Size About 15" (38 cm) wide across bottom, 13" (33 cm) wide across top opening, and 11" (28 cm) high after felting, not including strap and front flap closure.
Yarn CYCA #5 Bulky (chunky-weight) yarn: about 400 yd (366 m) main color (MC) and 75 yd (69 m) contrast color (CC). *Shown here:* Reynolds Lopi (100% Icelandic wool; 110 yd [100 m]/100 g): #0090 purple (MC), 4 skeins; about 75 yd (69 m) handspun, hand-dyed yarn (100% wool) by Holly Klump, mixed purple and pale yellow (CC).
Needles Size 10 (6 mm): 24" (60 cm) circular, and set of 2 double-pointed (dpn).
Notions Thick crochet cotton for provisional cast-on (used double); markers (m); tapestry needle; bath towel.
Gauge 17 sts and 30½ rnds = 4" (10 cm) in St st using MC, after felting; 13½ sts and 20 rows = 4" (10 cm) in broken checkerboard patt using CC, *not* felted. Your handspun yarn and gauge may vary.

for working in the rnd, being careful not to twist sts. *Set-up rnd:* With MC, p2, k11, p2, pm for side panel, p2, k36, p2, pm for front panel, p2, k11, p2 for other side panel, pm, p2, k36, p2 for back panel—15 sts for each side panel, 40 sts each for front and back panels. *Next rnd:* *P2, knit to 2 sts before next m, p2, slip m; rep from * to end of rnd. Rep the last rnd 15 more times—17 rnds total, including set-up rnd. *Next rnd:* *P2, k5, k1f&b (see Glossary, page 123), k5, p2, sl m, p2, k36, p2, sl m; rep from * once more—1 st inc'd in center of each side panel; 2 sts inc'd total. Work 1 rnd even (knit the knits, and purl the purls) without incs. Rep the last 2 rnds 10 more times—132 sts total: 26 sts for each side panel, still 40 sts each for front and back panels. Work 45 rnds even, or until piece measures about 14" (35.5 cm) from CO. Purl 5 rnds. Knit 1 rnd. BO all sts.

Top Edging
Remove crochet cotton from provisional CO along both side panels and front panel, and carefully place 70 live sts on needle as they become free, leaving 40 sts of back panel on provisional CO. With predominantly knit side facing, join CC to beg of sts for one side panel at top edge of bag. Knit 1 row, purl 1 row. BO all sts kwise.

Finishing
Turn bag inside-out so purl (rev St st) side of side, front, and back panels becomes the right, or public, side of the bag. Fold each 4-st column of knit sts in half to create vertical welts at each corner, and with MC threaded on a tapestry needle, use a backstitch (see Glossary, page 124) to sew the welts in place, stitching in the ditch where St st meets rev St st. Fold the 5-rnd section of St st at lower edge of bag in half to create a horizontal welt all around the lower edge, and with MC threaded on a tapestry needle, use a backstitch to sew the bottom welt as for side welts.

Bag Bottom
With MC, CO 45 sts. Work in seed stitch (see Stitch Guide) until panel measures the width of the side panels. BO all sts. With MC threaded on a tapes-

try needle, sew bag bottom into opening at lower (wider) edge of the bag, matching the four corners of the bottom piece to the four side welts.

Strap

Using MC and dpn, make three I-cords (see Glossary, page 123), each about twice as long as desired finished strap length. Braid the three cords together. With yarn threaded on a tapestry needle, sew each end of braided strap to inside of bag at center of each side panel. Weave in loose ends.

Felting

Place bag in mesh bag or pillow case to prevent strap from tangling in the agitator. Set washing machine for hot wash and cold rinse cycle and run bag through cycle until desired finished dimensions and appearance are achieved, checking frequently to prevent over-felting; your final results may vary from the bag shown here. Machine dry until nearly dry, then stuff with a towel to maintain shape and allow to air-dry thoroughly.

Flap

Remove crochet cotton from provisional CO and carefully place 40 live sts for back panel on needle. With RS facing, join CC and work across back sts as foll: [K3, k1f&b, p5] 2 times, k3, k1f&b, p4, p1f&b (see Glossary, page 124), p4, k3, k1f&b, p5—45 sts. Work in broken checkerboard patt (see Stitch Guide) for 40 rows—42 rows total including inc and set-up rows; flap measures about 8½" (21.5 cm). For a longer flap, keep working until flap reaches desired length, ending with Row 10 or Row 16 of patt, or until your handspun yarn runs out. BO all sts in patt. Weave in rem loose ends.

May Day Hat

Shannon Okey

My grandmother was Swedish, and in Sweden, *Midsommarsdag* celebrates the summer solstice with maypoles, food, and lots of fun. To spare you all from pronouncing *Midsommarsdag,* I've named this hat May Day, another celebration rife with maypoles. It's meant to look like the flower crowns (*blomkrans*) traditionally worn in young girls' hair; the wool daisies were spun right into the yarn by Tamara Lepianka of Houndscroft Farm.

Hat

With smaller cir needle and worsted yarn, CO 64 sts. Place marker (pm) and join for working in the rnd, being careful not to twist sts. Work k2, p2 rib for 5 rnds. *Next rnd:* Change to p2, k2 rib by purling the knit sts and knitting the purl sts. Work in newly established p2, k2 rib for 4 more rnds. Change back to k2, p2 rib work for 5 rnds—15 rnds completed in rib patts. Change to larger cir needle and bulky handspun yarn and purl 4 rnds. Change to smaller cir needle and worsted yarn and work 6 rnds in k2, p2 rib.

Crown

The crown is worked in the rnd in rev St st with worsted yarn. Dec as foll, changing to dpn when there are too few sts to fit comfortably on the cir needle.

Rnd 1: *K2tog, p2; rep from * to end of rnd—48 sts rem.

Rnd 2: Purl.

Rnd 3: *P2tog, p2; rep from * to end of rnd—36 sts rem.

Rnds 4 and 5: Purl.

Rnd 6: Rep Rnd 3—27 sts rem.

Rnds 7, 8, and 9: Purl.

Rnd 10: *P2tog, p2; rep from * to last 3 sts, p2tog, p1—20 sts rem.

Rnd 11: Purl.

Rnd 12: *P2tog, p2; rep from * to end of rnd—15 sts rem.

Rnd 13: [P2tog] 7 times, p1—8 sts rem.

Cut yarn, leaving a 10" (25.5 cm) tail.

Finishing

Thread tail on tapestry needle, draw through rem sts, pull tight to close top, and fasten off on WS. Weave in loose ends.

Finished Size About 19" (48.5 cm) head circumference with edge ribbing relaxed; will stretch to fit up to 22½" (57 cm).

Yarn CYCA #4 Medium (worsted-weight) yarn: about 100 yd [91 m]. CYCA #5 Bulky (chunky-weight) yarn: about 15 yd (14 m) handspun wool novelty yarn. *Shown here:* Brown Sheep Lamb's Pride Worsted (85% wool, 15% mohair; 190 yd [174 m]/113 g): #M191 kiwi, 1 skein. Handspun green novelty yarn with daisies (100% wool, about 3.5 to 4 wraps per inch) by Tamara Lepianka of Houndscroft Farm.

Needles Size 11 (8 mm): 16" (40 cm) circular (cir). Size 15 (10 mm): 16" (40 cm) cir and set of 4 or 5 double-pointed (dpn).

Notions Marker (m); tapestry needle.

Gauge 13½ sts and 20 rnds = 4" (10 cm) in k2, p2 rib worked in the rnd on smaller cir needle. Your handspun yarn and gauge may vary.

Birkeland Brothers Wool

(Cara and Norman Birkeland)

There's something to be said for a third-generation family fiber business founded on stubbornness! Birkeland Brothers Wool, owned by Norman Birkeland and his daughter Cara, owes its beginnings in part to an exasperated customs agent.

The Birkeland family worked in a Norwegian carding mill. When the mill shut down, its carders were sold for scrap metal. After exhausting their savings to buy two of the massive machines, Norman's father Olaf, uncle Mike, and their families immigrated to Vancouver, British Columbia, where they opened a wool shop that has remained in the same location since 1939.

When the carders arrived via ship, customs agents insisted the Birkelands pay duty, but Norman's father replied that because the machines were just scrap metal, he wouldn't pay duty—the agents could sink them in the port instead. (Cara notes her grandmother greatly objected to this tactic; after all, their entire savings had been invested in the machines!) But the family did leave without paying. One month later, the fees were waived just to get the family to take away the room-sized machines.

Today the Birkelands sell yarn, spinning wheels, and other retail items, but they are best known for their carded batts—still produced on the machines that nearly went to the bottom of the sea.

Visit the Birkeland Brothers website at
www.birkelandwool.net

Broken Cable Keyhole Scarf

Sue Jalowiec and Shannon Okey

This colorful scarf has "broken cable" motifs worked in handspun yarn. It is a great example of how to showcase small quantities of handspun/hand-dyed yarn. To allow for draw-in of the cable twists, stitches are increased at the beginning of the cables and decreased at the end of them. The natural-colored main yarn was spun by Judith Michels of Sithean Fibers, who has created a sanctuary for retired Corriedale ewes and other fibery creatures at her home in Wisconsin.

Stitch Guide

4/4RC

Slip 4 sts onto cable needle (cn) and hold in back of work, knit the next 4 sts, then the 4 sts from the cn.

Small Cable Motif with Color B in Front Cross

Row 1: (RS) K8 with MC, join A and work [k1f&b] 2 times (see Glossary, page 123), join B and work [k1f&b] 2 times, join separate ball of MC and k8—24 sts; 4 sts each in colors A and B; 8 sts at each end of row in MC.

Even-numbered Rows 2–10: (WS) K8 with MC, [p4 with color as it appears] 2 times, k8 with MC.

Rows 3 and 5: K8 with MC, k4 with A, k4 with B, k8 with MC.

Row 7: K8 with MC, work 4/4RC with colors as they appear (colors A and B exchange places at the cable crossing), k8 with MC.

Rows 9 and 11: K8 with MC, k4 with B, k4 with A, k8 with MC.

Row 12: Rep Row 2. Cut off A and B, leaving tails to weave in later.

Row 13: (RS) With a single ball of MC, k8, [k2tog] 4 times, k8—20 sts rem.

Finished Size 5" (12.5 cm) wide and 53" (134.5 cm) long.

Yarn CYCA #3 Light (DK-weight) yarn: about 210 yd (192 m) main color (MC). CYCA #4 Medium (worsted-weight) yarn: about 55 yd (50 m) color A and 20 yd (18 m) color B. *Shown here:* Natural-colored (beige) yarn by Judith Michels of Sithean Fibers (wool, mohair): about 60 grams (MC). Handspun, hand-dyed multicolor singles by Shannon Okey: pink/red mix (A), about 32 grams, and lime green (B), about 18 grams.

Needles Size 9 (5.5 mm): straight.

Notions Cable needle (cn); size J/10 (6 mm) crochet hook; tapestry needle.

Gauge 19 sts and 28½ rows = 4" (10 cm) in garter st with MC. Your handspun yarn and gauge may vary.

Small Cable Motif with Color A in Front Cross

Row 1: (RS) K8 with MC, join B and work [k1f&b] 2 times, join A and work [k1f&b] 2 times, join separate ball of MC and k8—24 sts; 4 sts each in colors A and B; 8 sts at each end of row in MC.

Even-numbered Rows 2-10: (WS) K8 with MC, [p4 with color as it appears] 2 times, k8 with MC.

Rows 3 and 5: K8 with MC, k4 with B, k4 with A, k8 with MC.

Row 7: K8 with MC, work 4/4RC with colors as they appear (colors A and B exchange places at the cable crossing), k8 with MC.

Rows 9 and 11: K8 with MC, k4 with A, k4 with B, k8 with MC.

Row 12: Rep Row 2. Cut off A and B, leaving tails to weave in later.

Row 13: (RS) With a single ball of MC, k8, [k2tog] 4 times, k8—20 sts rem.

Large Cable Motif

Row 1: (RS) K8 with MC, join A and work [k1f&b] 2 times, join B and work [k1f&b] 2 times, join separate ball of MC and k8—24 sts; 4 sts each in colors A and B; 8 sts at each end of row in MC.

Even-numbered Rows 2-22: (WS) K8 with MC, [p4 with color as it appears] 2 times, k8 with MC.

Rows 3 and 5: K8 with MC, k4 with A, k4 with B, k8 with MC.

Row 7: K8 with MC, work 4/4RC with colors as they appear (colors A and B exchange places at the cable crossing), k8 with MC.

Rows 9, 11, 13, 15, and 17: K8 with MC, k4 with B, k4 with A, k8 with MC.

Row 19: Rep Row 7 (colors A and B exchange places at cable crossing again).

Rows 21 and 23: Rep Row 3.

Row 24: Rep Row 2. Cut off A and B, leaving tails to weave in later.

Row 25: (RS) With a single ball of MC, k8, [k2tog] 4 times, k8—20 sts rem.

Scarf

With MC, CO 20 sts. Knit 9 rows, beg and end with a WS row—5 garter ridges. Work Rows 1-13 of small cable motif with color B in front cross (see Stitch Guide). Knit 7 rows, ending with a WS row. Work Rows 1-13 of small cable motif with color A in front cross (see Stitch Guide). Knit 7 rows. Work Rows 1-25 of large cable motif (see Stitch Guide). Knit 7 rows. Work Rows 1-13 of small cable motif with color B in front cross—piece measures about 13¼" (33.5 cm) from CO. Work even in garter st until piece measures about 35" (89 cm) from CO, ending with a WS row. Work keyhole as foll: With MC, k10, join a second ball of MC and k10. Working each side separately, cont even until piece measures 2½" (6.5 cm) from beg of keyhole. Break off second ball of MC and cont working across all sts with a single ball of yarn until piece measures 2½" (6.5 cm) from top of keyhole. Work Rows 1-13 of small cable motif with color A in front cross. Knit 7 rows. Work Rows 1-25 of large cable motif. Knit 7 rows. Work Rows 1-13 of small cable motif with color B in front cross. Knit 7 rows. Work Rows 1-13 of small cable motif with color A in front cross. Knit 9 rows, beg and ending with a WS row—5 garter ridges. Loosely BO all sts.

Finishing

Join A with RS facing to corner of scarf at beg of one long side. Using crochet hook, *work 1 sc (see Glossary, page 122) in each garter ridge of long side of scarf, 3 sc in corner, 18 sc across short end of scarf to next corner, 3 sc in corner; rep from * once more. Join to first sc with a slip st (see Glossary, page 122). Fasten off last st. Weave loose ends in behind their matching colors. Block lightly.

Power Station Hat

Shannon Okey

This is a very, very simple hat with an elegant look, thanks to overtwisted singles that cause the stockinette stitches to angle in various directions. The singles were spun from samples of Hatchtown Farm's Coopworth fiber in natural shades of grey and white; the decoration on the side is made from Houndscroft Farm silk-wrapped wool. I call this hat "Power Station" because it's so full of "energized" singles. This pattern is extremely flexible; depending on the yarn's weight, you can use any size needle from U.S. 6 to 10½. I've knitted more hats like this than I can count, and have never altered the number of stitches I cast on!

Finished Size About 20" (51 cm) head circumference with fabric relaxed and 8" (20.5 cm) tall.

Yarn CYCA #3 Light (DK-weight) singles: about 200 yd (183 m). *Shown here:* Handspun yarn by Shannon Okey, spun as highly overtwisted singles using three natural colors of Coopworth roving from Hatchtown Farm. About 1 yd (1 m) handspun silk-wrapped wool yarn by Houndscroft Farm for optional flower decoration.

Needles Size 9 (5.5 mm): 16" (40 cm) circular (cir) and set of 4 or 5 double-pointed (dpn).

Notions Marker (m); tapestry needle.

Gauge 16 sts and 28 rnds = 4" (10 cm) in St st with overspun yarn allowed to bias and with rnd gauge measured along a diagonal column of biased knit sts. Your handspun yarn and gauge may vary.

Hat

With cir needle, CO 80 sts. Place marker (pm) and join for working in the rnd, being careful not to twist sts. Work k2, p2 rib until piece measures 1" (2.5 cm). Work in rnds of stockinette, seed st, occasional rnds of 2-ply yarn, or other "overtwist-controlling" patt (see page 58), changing patts and colors randomly every 1–2" (2.5–5 cm) until piece measures 7" (18 cm) from CO.

Crown

Dec as foll, changing to dpn when there are too few sts to fit comfortably on cir needle.
Rnd 1: *K6, k2tog; rep from *–70 sts rem.
Even-numbered Rnds 2–12: Knit.
Rnd 3: *K5, k2tog; rep from *–60 sts rem.
Rnd 5: *K4, k2tog; rep from *–50 sts rem.

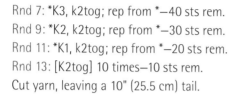

Rnd 7: *K3, k2tog; rep from *—40 sts rem.
Rnd 9: *K2, k2tog; rep from *—30 sts rem.
Rnd 11: *K1, k2tog; rep from *—20 sts rem.
Rnd 13: [K2tog] 10 times—10 sts rem.
Cut yarn, leaving a 10" (25.5 cm) tail.

Finishing

Thread tail on tapestry needle, draw through rem sts, pull tight to close top, and fasten off on WS. Weave in loose ends.

Flower

(optional) Wrap flower yarn about 4 times loosely around the fingers of one hand as if making a yarn butterfly. Wind one end tightly around the middle of the flower a few times to secure it, and tie ends together in a knot. With ends threaded on tapestry needle, attach to hat where desired, and fluff out loops into a flower shape.

Laura Jefferson and Sarah Dunham

You may already have a dye store in your backyard; Laura Jefferson and Sarah Dunham do! These crafty housemates have a large garden in the New Hampshire woods, filled with plants, flowers, cats, chickens, granite-loving lichens, and more. They enjoy dyeing with natural color sources, including indigo, lichens, and plant materials. In these photos, the pale purple color was obtained using lichens native to New England, and the blue came from indigo. You can see that while the fiber rests in the indigo pot, it looks green with an almost "oily" blue film on top. As soon as it comes out, though, it oxidizes in the air and turns the deep blue we think of as "indigo-colored." Check out Laura's Felted Mammoth Tea Cozy pattern on page 91; she's a dedicated archeologist who devotes much of each summer to Paleolithic-era digs near her home and has managed to combine both her interests in one project!

Felted Mammoth Tea Cozy

Laura Jefferson

To make this tea cozy, you first have to catch your mammoth. The way I went about this involved about 4 ounces of Romney roving from Mary Pratt at Elihu Farm in two shades of gray and my favorite handspindle. I spun a thick, fluffy singles in small cops, each containing about as much yarn as I felt like Andean plying in the same sitting, and plied it fairly loosely. The size of your tea cozy will likely have something to do with the size of your teapot, but since the object will be felted, there is a lot of wiggle room. The tea cozy is worked from the top down, with the hole for the teapot spout cut open after the mammoth has been felted.

Finished Size Can be customized to fit any tea-pot. Cozy shown measures about 26" (66 cm) circumference at lower edge and 7" (18 cm) tall, after felting, with lower edge rolled.

Yarn CYCA #5 Bulky (chunky-weight) yarn: about 150–200 yd (137–183 m). *Shown here:* Handspun yarn (100% Romney 2-ply wool): gray, about 4 oz (114 g).

Needles Size 13 or 15 (9 or 10 mm): 24" (60 cm) circular (cir), and set of 4 or 5 double-pointed (dpn).

Notions Markers (m); tapestry needle; 2-oz package of polymer clay in tusk color or one package each of two colors that can be blended for tusk color; strong cotton thread in matching color for attaching tusks.

Gauge None provided. Before beginning cozy, make a gauge swatch in St st using your chosen yarn and needles. Aim for a very loose, open fabric, and note the number of stitches per inch; the larger the stitches, the more room there will be for the yarn to shrink and felt into a dense fabric.

Note

Before felting, your finished cozy should be about one-third bigger around and one-third taller than your teapot. For example, if your teapot measures 26" (66 cm) around at the widest point and 7" (13.5 cm) tall, work the cozy to be about 34½" (87.5 cm) around and 9½" (24 cm) tall. The exact finished measurements can be fine-tuned during the felting process.

Cozy

With cir needle, CO enough sts to equal about 2" (5 cm) at your regular St st gauge, rounding up to an even number of sts. *Set-up row:* *K1f&b (see Glossary, page 123) in each st across—number of sts has doubled; still an even number of sts. Work 2 rows of double knitting as foll: *K1, sl 1 as if to purl with yarn in back (pwise wyb); rep from * to end. You have completed 2 rows total of double knitting, but each face of the fabric will appear as a single row of St st. Turn work so sts are on needle in your left hand with the working yarn at the tip of the needle. Hold 2 dpn in your right hand, and transfer sts from cir needle to 2 dpn as foll: *Sl 1 st to front dpn pwise, sl 1 st to back dpn pwise; rep from * to end—half the total number of sts transferred to each dpn. Distribute sts as evenly as possible on 3 or 4 dpn for working in the rnd. Knit 1 rnd, placing markers (pm) at the beg of rnd and at the halfway point so there are an equal number of sts in two sections between the markers (m). *Inc rnd:* *K1f&b, knit to 1 st before m, k1f&b; rep from * once more—4 sts inc'd. Work 3 or 4 rnds even in St st, then rep the inc rnd. Inc in this manner

every 4th or 5th rnd until the number of sts on the needles is enough to equal about one-third more than the circumference of your teapot (see Note). Work even in St st until piece is about one-third taller than desired height. For a tall, more cylindrical teapot, you might want to place the inc rnds closer together at the beg, then work a longer section even without incs. BO all sts.

Ears

For left ear, CO 1 st, and work a St st triangle as foll:
Row 1: (RS) K1f&b—2 sts.
Row 2: P1, p1f&b (see Glossary, page 124)—3 sts.
Row 3: K1f&b, knit to end—1 st inc'd.
Row 4: Purl to last st, p1f&b—1 st inc'd.
Cont in this manner, inc 1 st at beg of every RS row and end of every WS row, until there are enough sts to equal about 4½" (11.5 cm) wide at your gauge. BO all sts. For right ear, CO 1 st and work a mirror-image triangle as foll:
Row 1: (RS) K1f&b—2 sts.
Row 2: P1f&b, p1—3 sts.
Row 3: Knit to last st, k1f&b—1 st inc'd.
Row 4: P1f&b, purl to end—1 st inc'd.
Cont in this manner, inc 1 st at end of every RS row and beg of every WS row, until there are enough sts to equal about 4½" (11.5 cm) wide at your gauge. BO all sts.

Tail

With dpn, CO 3 sts. Work 3-st I-cord (see Glossary, page 123) until piece measures about 4" (10 cm) or one-third more than desired finished length. BO all sts.

Finishing

The 2 lines of incs on the body of the cozy correspond to the middle of the mammoth's face and the center of its backside. With yarn threaded on a tapestry needle, sew ears to head on either side of center line for face, and sew tail to body along center line of backside.

Felting

Felt cozy by hand or in the washing machine. For machine felting, place cozy in mesh bag or pillow case to prevent ears and tail from tangling in the agitator. Set washing machine for hot wash, cold rinse cycle, and run through multiple cycles as necessary until desired finished dimensions and appearance are achieved, checking frequently to prevent over-felting; your final results may vary from the cozy shown here. Place cozy on your teapot—the fabric will still have a little give while it is wet—and shape it to the desired final appearance. Leave cozy to dry on teapot to prevent it from shrinking.

Spout Hole

Cut a horizontal slit about 2" (5 cm) wide to accommodate the teapot spout. The heat and moisture of the hot tea in the teapot will further felt the cut ends and prevent them from raveling, but you may also reinforce the slit by sewing around the opening with yarn threaded on a tapestry needle.

Tusks

With tusk-colored polymer clay, or well-mixed blend of colors, make 2 clay snakes about 7" (18 cm) long and $\frac{1}{2}$" (1.3 cm) in diameter. Roll one end of each tusk into a point. Flatten the other end of each tusk slightly, and use tapestry needle to poke 2 holes through the tusk at the flattened end. Bake or cure the tusks according to the manufacturer's instructions. Don't worry if you overcook them a little; if they turn a little brown it will only enhance the look of the ancient ivory. With heavy cotton thread, sew one tusk to each side of face, on either side of the spout hole as shown.

Beauty School Dropout Pullover

Shoshana Matthews

Spin and ply a sportweight yarn from hair-dressers' coloring supplies! Hairdressers use loosely coiled unspun fiber to protect the face, neck, and ears from dripping dyes and perm liquids. You can buy it by the box in "roving" form in cotton or rayon from beauty supply houses.

Stitch Guide

Cloverleaf Eyelet Pattern (multiple of 8 sts + 7; from Barbara Walker's *A Treasury of Knitting Patterns*)
Row 1: (RS) Knit.
Row 2 and all even-numbered rows: (WS) Purl.
Row 3: K2, yo, sl 1, k2tog, psso, yo, *k5, yo, sl 1, k2tog, psso, yo; rep from * to last 2 sts, k2.

Finished Size 42½ (47½, 53)" (108 [120.5, 134.5] cm) bust circumference. Shown in size 53" (134.5 cm).

Yarn CYCA #2 Fine (sportweight) yarn: about 1250 (1375, 1550) yd (1143 [1257, 1417] m). *Shown here:* Handspun yarn by Shoshana Mathews (100% rayon 2-ply; CelluCotton Beauty Coil; 1200 ft [365 m]/box): white, 2 (2, 2) boxes.

Needles Size 4 (3.5 mm).

Notions Stitch holder; tapestry needle.

Gauge 24 sts and 35 rows = 4" (10 cm) in St st; 24 sts and 37 rows = 4" (10 cm) in cloverleaf eyelet patt; 22 sts and 32 rows = 4" (10 cm) in patt for sleeve. Your handspun yarn and gauge may vary.

Row 5: K3, yo, ssk, *k6, yo, ssk; rep from * to last 2
    sts, k2.

Row 7: Knit.

Row 9: K1, *k5, yo, sl 1, k2tog, psso, yo; rep from *
    to last 6 sts, k6.

Row 11: K7, *yo, ssk, k6; rep from *.

Row 12: Purl.

Repeat Rows 1–12 for pattern.

Back

CO 124 (140, 156) sts. Work k1, p1 rib until piece
measures 1¼" (3.2 cm) from CO, ending with a WS
row and inc 3 sts evenly in last row of rib—127 (143,
159) sts. Change to St st and work even until piece
measures 14 (14½, 15)" (35.5 [37, 38] cm) from CO,
ending with a WS row.

Shape Armholes

BO 5 (6, 7) sts at beg of next 2 rows—117 (131, 145)
sts rem. Cont in St st, dec 1 st each end of needle
every RS row 8 (10, 12) times—101 (111, 121) sts
rem. Cont even in St st until armholes measure 7¼
(7¾, 8¼)" (18.5 [19.5, 21] cm), ending with a WS
row.

Shape Back Neck

Next row: (RS) K33 (36, 39), join second ball of yarn
and BO center 35 (39, 43) sts, knit to end—33 (36,
39) sts at each side. Working each side separately,
work even in St st until armholes measure 8 (8½,
9)" (20.5 [21.5, 23] cm). BO all sts.

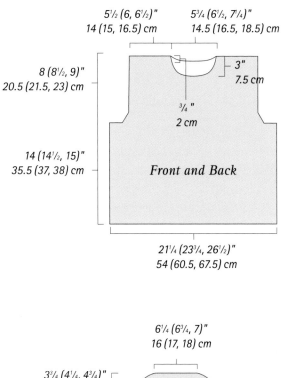

Front and Back

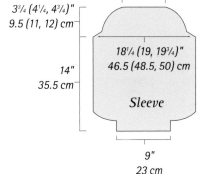

Sleeve

Front

CO 124 (140, 156) sts. Work k1, p1 rib until piece measures 1¼" (3.2 cm) from CO, ending with a WS row and inc 3 sts evenly in last row of rib—127 (143, 159) sts. Change to Cloverleaf Eyelet patt (see Stitch Guide) and work even in patt until piece measures 14 (14½, 15)" (35.5 [37, 38] cm) from CO, ending with a WS row.

Shape Armholes

BO 5 (6, 7) sts at beg of next 2 rows—117 (131, 145) sts rem. Cont in patt, dec 1 st each end of needle every RS row 8 (10, 12) times—101 (111, 121) sts rem. Cont even in patt until armholes measure 5 (5½, 6)" (12.5 [14, 15] cm), ending with a WS row.

Shape Front Neck

Next row: (RS) Work 39 (43, 47) sts in patt, place center 23 (25, 27) sts on holder, join second ball of yarn and work in patt to end—39 (43, 47) sts at each side. Working each side separately in patt, dec 1 st at each neck edge every RS row 6 (7, 8) times—33 (36, 39) sts rem at each side. Work even in patt until armholes measure 8 (8½, 9)" (20.5 [21.5, 23] cm). BO all sts.

Sleeves

CO 50 sts. Work k1, p1 rib until piece measures 1¾" (4.5 cm) from CO, ending with a WS row. *Next row:* (RS) K1f&b (see Glossary, page 123) in each st across—100 sts. Purl 1 WS row. Work patt for sleeve as foll:
Row 1: (RS) K2tog, yo; rep from * to end of row.
Rows 2, 3, and 4: Work 3 rows even in St st.
Rep these 4 rows once more—8 sleeve patt rows

completed. Beg with the next RS row, inc 1 st at each end of needle every 8 rows 0 (2, 4) times, working new sts into patt—100 (104, 108) sts. Work even in sleeve patt until piece measures 14" (35.5 cm) from CO, or desired length to armhole, ending with a WS row.

Shape Cap

BO 5 (6, 7) sts at beg of next 2 rows—90 (92, 94) sts rem. Dec 1 st each end of needle every RS row 11 times—68 (70, 72) sts rem; sleeve cap measures about 3" (7.5 cm). Cont even in patt, if necessary for your size, until sleeve cap measures 3 (3½, 4)" (7.5 [9, 10] cm), ending with a WS row. Change to St st, and BO 5 sts at beg of next 6 rows—38 (40, 42) sts rem; sleeve cap measures 3¾ (4¼, 4¾)" (9.5 [11, 12] cm). BO all sts.

Finishing

With yarn threaded on a tapestry needle, sew front to back at right shoulder.

Neckband

With RS facing at beg at right shoulder seam, pick up and knit 43 (47, 51) sts across back neck, pick up and knit 16 (17, 18) sts along left front neck, knit across 23 (25, 27) sts from front neck holder, pick up and knit 16 (17, 18) sts along right front neck—98 (106, 114) sts total. Work k1, p1 rib until neckband measures 2" (5 cm) from pick-up row. Loosely BO all sts. Sew rem shoulder and neckband seam. Fold neckband in half and sew BO edge of neckband to pick-up row on WS. Sew sleeve caps to armholes, then sew sleeve and side seams. Weave in loose ends. Block to measurements.

Catherine Goodwin

Catherine Goodwin invented the Spindolyn, a unique quill supported spindle made of two parts: a brass spindle whorl shaft and wooden base. The base features a specially shaped brass tube for the shaft to ride in while tucked comfortably into your lap, crossed knee, or between your feet. She's also developed her own sock yarn, and is an expert machine knitter.

Catherine lives in the countryside near Nashville, Tennessee, in a house with an antique barn, dogs, pawpaw trees, chickens, and an adorable donkey who grazes on the nearby hill. (There's poison ivy, too, I unfortunately discovered.) Catherine loves music; her boyfriend frequently plays the Nashville clubs, and she's been known to knit and spin while listening to his band. The Spindolyn can be used single-handedly, which is great when you're trying to drink coffee or pick up another bit of fiber from your basket without breaking your spinning rhythm.

Visit Catherine's website at
www.knittinganyway.com

Hatchtown Spindles

(Pam and Jim Child)

I should have known it the second I pulled out my camera—the gleam in his eye betrayed him. Jim Child is a former photographer turned shepherd, who raises Coopworth sheep with his wife Pam and their charming dogs on a small farm near the rocky Maine coastline. Skye, a border collie, is remarkably smart. When Pam asked him (without a single gesture; voice commands only) to take me behind the barn toward the pasture to capture photos of the sheep switching locations, he immediately complied— even giving me a funny look when I didn't start walking right away.

When Jim's not feeding the sheep, he's turning his own kind of wheel—a lathe—to produce unique spindles and fiber tools, similar to Russian lace spindles (sometimes called Orenburg spindles after the ethereal, thin shawls made from their efforts). No hook, no whorl, just a gently tapered shaft of wood that spins very quickly, giving just the right amount of twist to cobweb-weight fibers.

Pam's in charge of the fiber side of the business, and she produces prizewinning Coopworth fleeces with excellent handspinning properties. It's clear the sheep appreciate her work—on the day of my visit, the last bottle lamb followed her around the pens, begging for attention.

Visit the Hatchtown Spindles website at
www.hatchtownfarm.com

Mojave Socks

Erin O'Brien

I like knitting toe-up socks as a relatively new spinner because I don't need to worry about wraps per inch (WPI; see Glossary, page 126) and if I overspin the yarn a bit, it will just wear longer and felt a little less. All good things! I learned short-row toes and heels from one of my knitting gurus, Anne Claxon, and rarely use anything else in my socks because it's so easy to make a sock that fits. Knitting from the toe up allows you to try the sock on as you go to double check the fit.

Notes

- If only one number appears in the instructions it refers to both sizes.
- When working this type of short-row toe, work only the stitches in between the wrapped stitches. Visit www.knitty.com for an excellent article on short-row toes and heels with illustrations, "Tiptop Toes," by Wendy D. Johnson.
- You can choose to work the entire sock in the same yarn throughout and you can substitute your favorite rib pattern for the cabled rib shown here.

Finished Size About 8" (20.5 cm) foot circumference and 8½ (9½)" (21.5 [24] cm) long from back of heel to tip of toe; to fit woman's U.S. shoe size 6 to 7½ (8 to 9). Socks shown in 8½" (21.5 cm) length.

Yarn CYCA #2 Fine (sportweight) yarn: about 280 (320) yd (256 [293] m) main color (MC) for leg and foot; 80 yd (73 m) contrast color (CC) for toe and heel. *Shown here:* Handspun 100% wool yarn by Erin O'Brien, Ashland Bay Merino Top Multi-color in Mojave (MC) and brown Border Leicester roving plied with Mojave Merino Top (CC).

Needles Size 2 (2.75 mm): set of 5 double-pointed (dpn).

Notions Waste yarn for provisional cast-on; marker (m); cable needle (cn); tapestry needle.

Gauge 11½ sts and 16 rnds = 2" (5 cm) in St st, worked in the rnd. Your handspun yarn and gauge may vary.

- Spin up about 360 (400) yd (329 [366] m) of yarn total—more if your yarn is very fine, less if it's bulkier. I generally use a 3-ply yarn for its increased strength and because it doesn't bias the way a single-ply yarn might. For the toe and heel of the socks shown, I used one ply of merino and two plies of Border Leicester for durability. For the rest of the sock, I used merino in all three plies for softness. Using a different yarn for the toes and heels has the added bonus that it's easy to identify which stitches are part of a toe or heel if they wear out and need to be replaced.
- Knit a swatch. This should ideally be in the round (does a friend need a wristband?) because the socks will be worked in the round. Aim for a stretchy but very dense fabric, which is what I like in my socks, but feel free to play around with the gauge of your own yarn until you're happy.
- Measure around the widest part of the ball of the wearer's foot and multiply that measurement by your gauge to determine how many stitches you need for the foot. The other key measurement you need is the length of the wearer's foot which you will use to decide when to start the heel.

Toe

With CC and using the provisional method (see Glossary, page 122), CO 23 sts, or half the total desired number of foot sts.

First Half

With A, work short-rows (see Glossary, page 125) as foll:

Row 1: (RS) K22, wrap the last st, turn work.

Row 2: (WS) P21, wrap the last st, turn—21 sts between wrapped sts; 1 wrapped st at each end of row.

Row 3: K20 (1 st before the previous wrapped st), wrap the next st, turn.

Row 4: P19 (1 st before the previous wrapped st), wrap the next st, turn—19 sts between wrapped sts; 2 wrapped sts at each end of row.

Cont in this manner, working 1 less st before wrapping and turning every row until 9 sts rem between wrapped sts, ending with a WS purl row—7 wrapped sts at each end of row.

TIP

If you have pointy toes, cont working short-rows until 5 or 7 sts rem between wrapped sts; if you have wide toes, work short-rows until there are 11 sts between wrapped sts.

Second Half

Cont as foll:

Row 1: (RS) K9 (to the first wrapped st), knit the wrapped st tog with its wrap, wrap the next st (this st is now wrapped twice), turn.

Row 2: (WS) P10 (to the first wrapped st), purl wrapped st tog with its wrap, wrap the next st (this st is now wrapped twice), turn.

Row 3: K11 (to the twice-wrapped st), knit wrapped st tog with both its wraps, wrap the next st, turn.

Row 4: P12 (to the twice-wrapped st), purl wrapped st tog with both its wraps, wrap the next st, turn.

Cont in this manner until you have worked the last double-wrapped st at each side tog with both wraps, ending with a WS row—23 sts. If you have adjusted the st count and ended on a RS row, purl 1 WS row across all sts.

Foot

Divide sts as evenly as possible between 2 dpn. Carefully remove waste yarn from base of provisional CO and place the 23 exposed live sts on 2 additional dpn—46 sts total; 23 sts on 2 dpn for the top of foot; 23 sts on 2 dpn for bottom of foot. *Note:* It is important to maintain the sts in these two sets so you can later align the heel with the toe. Place marker (pm) and join for knitting in the rnd; rnd beg at side of foot where working yarn is attached. Knit 1 rnd even. Change to MC. Knit even until piece measures 6¼ (7¼)" (16 [18.5] cm), or 2¼" (5.5 cm) less than total desired foot length, ending at marker at side of foot.

Heel

First Half

Change to CC. Work short-rows on first 23 sts of rnd (or first half of your total sts) as for first half of toe, beg with Row 1. Cont as for toe until 7 sts rem between wrapped sts, ending with a WS purl row—8 wrapped sts at each end of row.

Second Half

Cont as for second half of toe, beg by working to the first wrapped st in first RS row. Cont as for toe

until you have worked the last double-wrapped st at each side tog with both its wraps, ending with a WS row. If you have adjusted the st count and ended on a RS row, purl 1 WS row across heel sts.

Leg

Change to MC and resume working St st in the rnd on all 46 sts until piece measures 1½" (3.8 cm) from last heel row, or to the top of the ankle bone. *Next rnd:* *[K2, k1f&b (see Glossary, page 123)] 3 times, k3, k1f&b; rep from * 2 more times, k2, k1f&b, k3, k1f&b—60 sts. Rearrange sts if necessary into 2 groups of 30 sts. Work cable patt as foll:

Rnd 1: *P2, k4; rep from *.

Rnd 2: (cable crossing rnd) *P2, sl 2 sts onto cn and hold in front, k2, k2 from cn; rep from *.

Rnds 3–8: Rep Rnd 1 six times.

Rnd 9: Rep Rnd 2.

Rnds 10–16: Rep Rnds 3–9 once.

Rnds 17–20: Rep Rnd 1 four times.

Rnd 21: Rep Rnd 2.

Rnds 22–27: Rep Rnd 1 six times.

Rnd 28: Rep Rnd 2.

Rnds 29–33: Rep Rnd 17–21 once.

Rnds 34–51: Rep Rnds 3–20 once more—piece measures about 9" (23 cm) from bottom of heel.

Loosely BO all sts.

Finishing

Weave in loose ends. Block lightly.

Elaine Evans

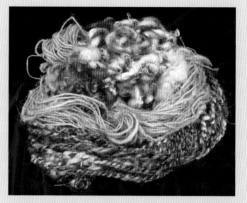

Elaine Evans lives in Minnesota, where her line of Fuzzy Bumblebee yarns keep her warm throughout the winter. She often collaborates with Ana Voog, known for her outrageous, beautiful free-form crochet hats, some of which include Elaine's yarn. Elaine crochets, too—unusual organic shapes that are dictated by what the yarn tells her to do. I've often said that the yarn designs as much as the human behind the needles, and Elaine's work is a prime example. Elaine hand-dyes the fibers she uses in her yarns and projects, including luminous chartreuse Lincoln locks, multicolor wools, and more.

Visit Elaine's website at www.fuzzybumblebee.com

Orangina Scarf

Jillian Moreno for Acme Knitting Company

Two, two, two scarves in one! Wrap it lacy or wrap it ruffly. The stay-closed, stay-put button closure gets extra points for letting you raid your vintage button stash. This versatile scarf suits any amount of handspun—it could be knitted entirely in handspun, or just the ruffle, or just the edgings. Spin it and knit it your way.

Finished Size 4½" (11.5 cm) wide and 53¾" (136.5 cm) long, including ruffle and picot edgings.

Yarn CYCA #4 Medium (worsted-weight) yarn: about 315 yd (288 m) main color (MC). CYCA #5 Bulky (chunky-weight) yarn: about 100 yd (91 m) for ruffles (CC). *Shown here:* Malabrigo Merino (100% merino wool; 215 yd [196 m]/100 g) Mandarina (MC), 2 skeins; and handspun, hand-dyed yarn by Sandra Durkin of Snapcrafty.com (100% Falklands wool; 102 yd [93 m]/3.3 oz; about 7 wraps per inch): cinnamon apple pie (CC), 1 skein.

Needles Size 9 (5.5 mm): straight. Size 10½ (6.5 mm): 24" (60 cm) circular (cir).

Notions Tapestry needle; one 1½" (3.8 cm) button.

Gauge 18 sts and 18 rows = 4" (10 cm) in Shetland garter lace with MC on smaller needles, after blocking; 18 sts and 19 rows = 4" (10 cm) in double moss st with MC on smaller needles, after blocking. Your handspun yarn and gauge may vary.

Stitch Guide

Shetland Garter Lace (multiple of 4 sts)

Row 1: (RS) *K2tog, yo twice, k2tog; rep from * to end of row.

Row 2: (WS) *K1, (k1, p1) into double yo of previous row, k1; rep from * to end of row.

Row 3: K2, *k2tog, yo twice, k2tog; rep from * to last 2 sts, end k2.

Row 4: K2, *k1, (k1, p1) into double yo of previous row, k1; rep from * to last 2 sts, end k2.

Repeat Rows 1–4 for pattern.

Double Moss Stitch (multiple of 4 sts)

Rows 1 and 2: *K2, p2; rep from * to end of row.

Rows 3 and 4: *P2, k2; rep from * to end of row.

Repeat Rows 1–4 for pattern.

Scarf

With MC and smaller needles, CO 20 sts. Work in Shetland garter lace (see Stitch Guide) for 118 rows, ending with Row 2 of patt. Change to double moss st (see Stitch Guide) and work even for 112 rows, ending with Row 4 of patt. *Buttonhole row:* (RS) Work 8 sts in patt, k2tog, yo twice, k2tog, work 8 sts in patt. *Next row:* (WS) Work 9 sts in patt, work k1, p1 in double yo of previous row, work 9 sts in patt. Work 2 rows in established patt across all sts, ending with Row 4 of patt—116 rows total in double moss st. Loosely BO all sts.

Finishing

Wet block scarf so Shetland garter lace section measures 6" (15 cm) wide and 27½" (70 cm) long, and double moss section measures 5" (12.5 cm) wide and 26½" (67.5 cm) long. Scarf will relax to about 4½" (11.5 cm) wide and 50¾" (129 cm) long.

Picot Edging

With CC, larger cir needle, and RS facing, pick up and knit 20 sts evenly spaced along CO edge of Shetland garter lace patt. Work garter st (knit every row) for 4 rows. Using the picot edge method, BO as foll: *Use the knitted method (see Glossary, page 121) to CO 2 sts onto left-hand needle, BO 4 sts, slip rem st back onto left needle; rep from * until all sts have been BO, alternating casting on 2 sts and binding off 4 sts until 1 st rem. Fasten off last st.

Ruffle Edging

With CC, larger cir needle, and RS facing, pick up and knit 14 sts along BO edge of double moss st section. Cont as foll:

Row 1: (WS) P1f&b (see Glossary, page 124) in each st across—28 sts.

Row 2: (RS) K1f&b (see Glossary, page 123) in each st across—56 sts.

Rows 3, 4, and 5: Work 3 rows even in St st (knit on RS, purl on WS).

BO all sts.

Center Ruffle

With CC, larger cir needle, RS facing, and beg in center of 10th row of double moss st, pick up and knit 49 sts evenly along centerline of double moss stitch section, ending 2 rows before beg of buttonhole. Cont as foll:

Row 1: (WS) P1f&b in each st across—98 sts.

Row 2: (RS) K1f&b in each st across—196 sts.

Rows 3, 4, and 5: Work 3 rows even in St st.

BO all sts. Sew button in center of scarf on the first row of double moss st. Weave in loose ends.

Copper Moose Shawl

Crystal Canning

Designer Crystal Canning died before this pattern was written out (see page 108), so I've named it after her business, which continues under her husband's direction. Heather Brack puzzled out the lace pattern and counted the enormous number of stitches around the edge. We were both amazed by the simple yet elegant construction techniques used. This was one of many lightweight yet warm shawls knit by Crystal in the year preceding her accident—she seemed to have drawers full of them! Its soft natural brown color is flattering to almost anyone.

Finished Size About 56" (142 cm) square, after blocking.

Yarn CYCA #1 Super Fine (fingering-weight) yarn: about 2150 yd (1966 m). *Shown here:* Handspun 2-ply yarn by Crystal Canning (100% wool; about 16 wraps per inch) in natural brown, about 260 grams.

Needles Size 8 (5 mm): two 24" (60 cm) circular (cir). One size 8 (5 mm): straight or double-pointed (dpn) for working edging.

Notions Markers (m); tapestry needle.

Gauge 14 sts and 31 rows = 4" (10 cm) in garter stitch, after blocking. Your handspun yarn and gauge may vary.

Notes

- The center square of the shawl is made up of two triangles that are grafted together along the diagonal of the square.
- Each time you repeat Rows 27–40 of the Center chart you will have added enough stitches to work an additional repeat on each side of the center stitch(es). For example, the second time you work Rows 27–40, work the stitches before the first outlined repeat once, work the first outlined repeat two times, work the center stitch(es) between the repeats once, work the second outlined repeat two times, then work the stitches after the second repeat once to end.
- When working the border, make sure the markers do not accidentally slip underneath the yarnovers and migrate into the wrong positions. The markers should remain next to the corner stitches throughout.

Shawl

Center Panels

With cir needle, CO 3 sts. Purl 1 row. Work Rows 1–40 of Center chart once—43 sts. Rep Rows 27–40 *only* 7 more times (see Notes)—141 sts. Work Rows 27–32 once more—147 sts. Cut yarn and leave live sts on needle. For second center panel, work as before, ending 1 row earlier with RS Row 31—also 147 sts.

Join Center Panels

To graft the center panels invisibly in garter st, hold the needle with the first center panel in front with RS facing; this should be the piece with purl bumps from the previous WS row up against the needle. Hold the needle with the second panel behind the first needle so the wrong sides of the two pieces face each other. The grafting row will supply the final WS row that you omitted from the second panel. With yarn threaded on a tapestry needle, graft the live sts in garter st to form a square as foll:

Step 1: Insert tapestry needle into first st on front needle as if to purl and leave st on needle.

Step 2: Insert tapestry needle into first st on back needle as if to purl and leave st on needle.

Step 3: Insert tapestry needle into first st on front needle as if to knit and slip st from needle; insert tapestry needle into next st on front needle as if to purl and leave st on needle.

Step 4: Insert tapestry needle into first st on back needle as if to knit and slip st from needle; insert tapestry needle into next st on back needle as if to purl and leave st on needle.

Rep Steps 3 and 4 until all sts have been joined.

Border

With RS facing, join yarn to corner of center square. *Pick up and knit 1 st in corner of center square, place marker (pm), pick up and knit 89 sts along one side of center square (about 6 sts for every 10 rows or 5 garter ridges), pm; rep from * 3 more times (you may find it helpful to use a different color for the last marker to indicate the end of rnd)—360 sts total. Join for working in the rnd. Work in garter st as foll:

Rnd 1: Purl.

Rnd 2: (inc rnd) *K1 (corner st), slip marker (sl m), yo, knit to next marker, yo, sl m; rep from * 3 more times—8 sts inc'd.

Rep these 2 rnds 18 more times, changing to 2 cir needles if there are too many sts to fit comfortably on a single cir needle—512 sts. Purl 1 more rnd, removing markers as you come to them—20 garter ridges completed from pick-up rnd. Do not BO.

Edging

With a spare straight needle or dpn and RS of shawl facing, use the knitted method (see Glossary, page 121) to CO 18 sts onto left needle. Rep Rows 1–16 of Edging chart a total of 64 times, joining edging to shawl by working the last st of every RS edging row as k2tog with 1 live st from shawl border—18 edging sts rem; all live sts from border have been joined.

Finishing

With yarn threaded on a tapestry needle, use the Kitchener stitch (see Glossary, page 125) to graft the rem 18 live border sts to base of edging CO. Wet-block to finished measurements, using blocking wires and/or pins. Weave in loose ends.

k on RS

• k on WS

○ yo

╱ k2tog

⅄ k3tog

pattern repeat

Center

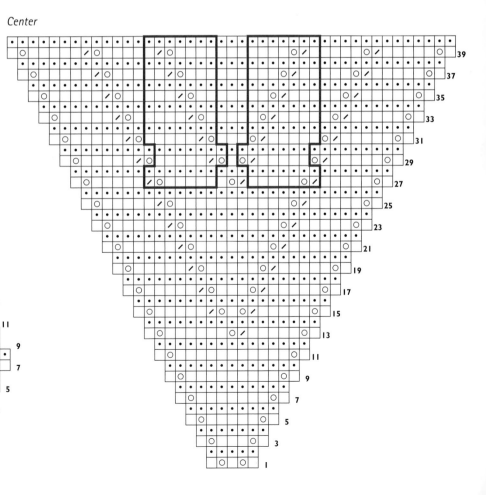

Edging

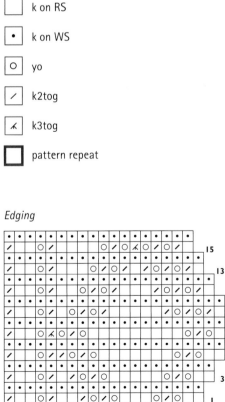

Crystal Canning

Crystal Canning owned Copper Moose in Vermont, a supplier of fine fibers, wheels, and more to the spinning community. She passed away after a tragic accident less than two months after these photos were taken. Copper Moose, however, continues under her husband's direction. Crystal was well known for her wicked sense of humor and unfailing patience with beginning spinners, always taking the time to make sure they had exactly what they needed to get started successfully.

To get a sense of Crystal's working environment, imagine this: outside, a mohair goat (who spends his time mowing the hillside and snacking on pine needles), chickens, tomatoes, and the green Vermont countryside. Inside the house, spinning wheels were everywhere. Crystal had quite a collection of featherweight handspun, handknitted shawls, many of which she made while recovering from a car accident the previous year. The Copper Moose shawl on page 105 even won prizes at her local fair.

Visit the Copper Moose website at www.coppermoose.com

Grow Hat

Lexi Boeger for Pluckyfluff

Lexi knitted this hat, but she didn't write down the pattern as she went along, so I've reverse-engineered it for you. What's crucial for a pattern as simple as this one is to use really interesting yarn. It needs texture, it needs wooly pieces flying out on all sides, it needs someone with a daring personality to wear it afterwards. But the actual hat is very simple.

> Finished Size About 21" (53.5 cm) circumference and 8" (20.5 cm) tall with lower edge rolled.
> Yarn CYCA #5 Bulky (chunky-weight) yarn: about 110 yd (100 m). *Shown here:* Hand-spun yarn by Lexi Boeger of Pluckyfluff (100% wool and various wool blends) in lengths of solid-color singles alternating with lengths of multicolored novelty singles.
> Needles Size 13 (9 mm): 16" (40 cm) circular (cir) and set of 4 or 5 double-pointed (dpn).
> Notions Marker (m); tapestry needle.
> Gauge About 10½ sts and 20 rnds = 4" (10 cm) in St st worked in the rnd. Your handspun yarn and gauge may vary.

Note

You can achieve an effect similar to the yarn shown here by working the stockinette stitch knit rounds in a plain yarn and the reverse stockinette stitch purl rounds in a wild, textured yarn. You can also add some odds and ends of handspun yarn or unspun fiber to the reverse stockinette stitch bands. Locks of Lincoln wool or mohair are great for this—knit the end of each lock or short length of yarn together with the main yarn for a few stitches to anchor the embellishment in place.

Brim

CO 55 sts. Place marker (pm) and join for working in the rnd, being careful not to twist sts. Work in bands of stockinette and reverse stockinette stitch as foll.

Rnds 1–4: Knit 4 rnds.
Rnds 5–8: Purl 4 rnds.
Rnds 9–19: Knit 11 rnds.
Rnds 20–23: Purl 4 rnds.

Rnds 24–26: Knit 3 rnds.

Rnds 27–28: Purl 2 rnds.

Rnds 29–37: Knit 9 rnds.

Rnds 38–40: Purl 3 rnds—piece measures about 8" (20.5 cm) from CO with lower edge unrolled.

Top

Dec as foll:

Rnd 1: *K2tog, k2; rep from * to last 3 sts, k2tog, k1—41 sts rem.

Rnd 2 and all even-numbered rnds: Knit.

Rnd 3: *K2tog, k2; rep from * to last st, k1—31 sts rem.

Rnd 5: *K2tog, k2; rep from * to last 3 sts, k2tog, k1—23 sts rem.

Rnd 7: *K2tog, k2; rep from * to last 3 sts, k2tog, k1—17 sts rem.

Rnd 9: *K2tog, k2; rep from * to last st, k1—13 sts rem.

Rnd 11: *K2tog, k2; rep from * to last st, k1—10 sts rem.

Cut yarn, leaving a 10" (25.5 cm) tail.

Finishing

Thread tail on tapestry needle, draw through rem sts, pull tight to close top, and fasten off on WS. Weave in loose ends.

Lexi Boeger

Lexi Boeger recently self-published a book called *Handspun Revolution* (Pluckyfluff, 2005), an apt title, given what she does. She's the Madonna of spinning; love her art or hate it, you've got to admit she has a gift for reinventing what comes off the wheel. Yarns with intentionally placed overspun coils, yarns with pom-poms or felted "nubbles" incorporated directly (no need to knit a bobble when you've got a bobble on the yarn), yarns with dreadlocks, with seashells, with tiny spiders—she rarely spins the same thing twice. And that's okay!

Lexi started the hard way: with a filthy raw fleece, handcards, and a drop spindle. The owner of her local yarn store (Lofty Lou's) in Placerville, California, taught her the basics. Lexi spun a lot of straight, even yarn before she learned to "go crooked." She believes you have to learn the rules in order to break them, and that serendipitous mistakes can be your best friend. You can see Lexi's yarn used in the Grow Hat (knitted by Lexi herself) at left and Garter Scarf 2 on page 61. Under the business name Pluckyfluff, Lexi sells yarn and various finished knitted items online (www.pluckyfluff.com).

Star Wristlets

Shannon Okey

These wristlets were inspired by Sivia Harding's amazing beaded knits. The ruffle is made of spindle-spun cantaloupe-colored wool from Sheila Bosworth (see page 112); it's light and airy, where the wristlets themselves are nice and warm. They don't take a lot of yarn to make and can be worn year round if you happen to work in a chilly office or a cold climate. (I wish I'd had them with me in San Francisco last summer!)

> Finished Size About 6" (15 cm) wrist circumference with ribbing relaxed and 4" (10 cm) long including ruffle; will stretch to fit up to 8" (20.5 cm) circumference.
> Yarn CYCA #1 Super Fine (fingering-weight) yarn: about 115 yd (105 m) main color (MC) and 90 yd (82 m) contrast color (CC). *Shown here:* Lanet Superwash (100% merino; 216 yd [198 m]/50 g): #1012 off-white, 1 ball (MC); yarn distributed by Norwegian Spirit. Handspun wool laceweight yarn spindle-spun by Sheila Bosworth in cantaloupe color.
> Needles Size 0 (2 mm): straight.
> Notions 46 silver star beads; Big-Eye beading needle for threading beads on yarn (available at bead and craft stores); tapestry needle.
> Gauge About 16½ sts and 17 rnds = 2" (5 cm) in k1, p1 rib with fingering-weight yarn. Your handspun yarn and gauge may vary.

Stitch Guide

Slip Stitch and Place Bead (SPB)
With yarn in front, slip next knit st pwise and slide bead into place in front of slipped st.

Wristlet

Using a Big-Eye beading needle, thread 46 beads onto MC (23 beads for each cuff). Using the provisional method (see Glossary, page 122), CO 50 sts.

Rows 1–4: Work in k1, p1 rib for 4 rows, ending with a WS row.

Row 5: (RS; bead row) [K1, p1] 6 times, *SPB (see Stitch Guide), [p1, k1] 2 times, p1; rep from * 3 more times, SPB, [p1, k1] 6 times, p1.

Rows 6–10: Work in established rib for 5 rows, ending with a WS row.

Row 11: (RS; bead row) [K1, p1] 7 times, SPB, [p1, k1] 3 times, p1, SPB, p1, k1, p1, SPB, [p1, k1] 3 times, p1, SPB, [p1, k1] 7 times, p1.

Rows 12–16: Work in established rib for 5 rows, ending with a WS row.

Rows 17–28: Rep Rows 5–16 once more—4 bead rows completed after Row 23.

Row 29: Rep Row 5—5 bead rows completed.

Row 30: Work 1 WS row even in established rib—piece measures about 3½" (9 cm) from CO.

Finishing

Ruffle

Change to CC and knit 1 RS row. Work in garter st as foll:

Row 1: K1f&b (see Glossary, page 123) in each st across row—100 sts.

Rows 2 and 4: Knit.

Row 3: Rep Row 1—200 sts.

Row 5: Rep Row 1—400 sts.

BO all sts.

Plain Edge

Carefully remove waste yarn from provisional CO and place 50 live sts on needle. Join CC with RS facing and BO all sts knitwise.

With yarn threaded on a tapestry needle, sew side seam. Weave in loose ends.

Jonathan and Sheila Bosworth

Jonathan Bosworth is a second-generation fiber artist; his parents, Ed and Helen Bosworth, were well-known weavers, and Ed made looms as well as other fiber tools. Under his father's supervision, Jonathan made his first charkha wheel in 1957 for a state fair in New York, and won a prize for his artistry. A charkha is a small Indian wheel enclosed in a case—it's the wheel in the famous photo of Mahatma Gandhi spinning cotton.

Many years later, Jonathan continues to craft amazing fiber tools. His Journey Wheel is an adapted charkha design that features a treadle and flyer instead of the more traditional hand crank and quill. In just four years, he has single-handedly built nearly 650 charkhas of various sizes, as well as Journey Wheels, and more than 3,000 drop spindles.

And what drop spindles they are! Rare and unusual woods, moose antlers, woolly mammoth tusks and mammoth teeth (the latter two have waiting lists of patient customers a mile long). If you've never seen a mammoth tusk in person, prepare to be surprised: the most descriptive colors sound like choices at a coffee bar: mocha, café au lait, and vanilla.

Sheila came late to spinning, although she's a longtime quilter and seamstress of historical costumes. She claims she learned to spin "in self-defense" after attending a couple of fiber festivals, but she now appreciates the portability of spindle spinning. Sheila's often on the road with the musicians she coaches (she's an expert in early music); spinning gives her time to unwind, if you'll pardon the reverse pun.

Visit their website at www.journeywheel.com

Firecracker Hat

Shannon Okey

When I say I don't throw anything away, I mean I really don't throw anything away. This hat offers a great way to use up some handspun or other precious scraps of yarn. It begins, essentially, with a sleeve shape. Experiment with your yarn of choice and personal gauge . . . this pattern is very flexible.

Finished Size About 22 (23½)" (56 [59.5] cm) head circumference and about 9" (23 cm) tall with lower edge rolled.

Yarn CYCA #4 Medium (worsted-weight) yarn: about 180 (190) yd (165 [174 m]), and odds and ends of various leftover yarns for fringe. *Shown here:* Brown Sheep Lamb's Pride Worsted (85% wool, 15% mohair; 190 yd [174 m]/114 g): #M180 ruby red, 1 (1) skein. Fringe yarns of various fibers and weights from Shannon's yarn stash.

Needles Size 10½ (6.5 mm): 16" (40 cm) circular (cir) and set of 4 or 5 double-pointed (dpn).

Notions Marker (m); tapestry needle; size G/6 (4.25 mm) crochet hook for applying fringe.

Gauge 15 sts and 23 rnds = 4" (10 cm) in St st worked in the rnd. Your handspun yarn and gauge may vary.

Notes

- This hat is worked in stockinette stitch in the round, then turned inside out so that the reverse stockinette stitch side is the "public" side.
- To adjust the height of the hat, work more or fewer 4-round decrease sequences before beginning the crown shaping. Every 4 rounds added or removed will lengthen or shorten the hat by about ¾" (2 cm). Be generous—this hat looks good somewhat longer than average, like an old-fashioned night cap.

Hat

CO 82 (88) sts. Place marker (pm) and join for working in the rnd, being careful not to twist sts. Knit 5 rnds. *Dec rnd:* K1, k2tog, knit to last 3 sts of rnd, k2tog through back loops (tbl), k1—2 sts dec'd. Knit 3 rnds. Rep the last 4 rnds 12 more times, or as many times as desired if adjusting length (see Notes)—56 (62) sts rem; piece measures about 10" (25.5 cm) from CO edge. Purl 1 rnd, dec 0 (2) sts as you go—56 (60) sts rem.

Crown

Dec as foll, changing to dpn when there are too few sts to fit comfortably on cir needle:
Rnd 1: *K2tog, k2; rep from * to end—42 (45) sts rem.
Rnd 2 and all even-numbered rnds: Knit.
Rnd 3: *K2tog, k2; rep from * to last 2 (1) st(s), [k2tog] 1 (0) time, k0 (1)—31 (34) sts rem.
Rnd 5: *K2tog, k2; rep from * to last 3 (2) sts, k2tog, k1 (0)—23 (25) sts rem.
Rnd 7: *K2tog, k2; rep from * to last 3 (1) st(s), [k2tog] 1 (0) time, k1—17 (19) sts rem.
Rnd 9: *K2tog, k2; rep from * to last 1 (3) st(s), [k2tog] 0 (1) time, k1—13 (14) sts rem.

Rnd 11: *K2tog, k2; rep from * to last 1 (2) st(s), [k2tog] 0 (1) time, k1 (0)—10 sts rem for both sizes.
Rnd 13: *K2tog; k2; rep from * to last 2 sts, k2tog—7 sts rem.
Cut yarn, leaving a 10" (25.5 cm) tail.

Finishing

Thread tail on tapestry needle, draw through rem sts, pull tight to close top, and fasten off on WS. Weave in loose ends. Turn hat inside out so that the "purl" side is the "public" side.

Fringe

Cut accent yarns into 56 (60) strands, each about 8-10" (20.5-25.5 cm) long. The purl ridge worked just before the crown shaping will appear as a knit rnd on the "public" side of the hat. Using a crochet hook, apply fringe around top of hat along knit rnd as foll: Fold a fringe strand in half, use crochet hook to pull loop through knit rnd st, pull the yarn ends through the loop, and tighten. Apply a fringe strand in this manner to every st in the knit rnd.

TIP

Applying fun fringe as a special accent is not limited to this hat. You could also use it on a collar, a wristlet, a button band—anywhere you'd like some extra texture and an interesting visual effect. It even works with felted bags; simply add the fringe in nonfelting strips of yarn before you felt the bag, or use a sharp tapestry needle to attach strands after felting.

Chillicothe

I enjoy rescuing neglected Shetlands from the thrift store; if they've got a hole, that's okay—I can knit over it to add more color! I call this sweater "Chillicothe" because the loops around the neck look like the Native American serpent mounds near that city in southern Ohio—a quarter-mile-long, undulating serpent mound, the largest of its kind in the United States. This project does not include directions for making the sweater body. Start with a thrift shop pullover in the right size and follow the instructions below to convert it into an embellished cardigan like the one shown.

Finished Size Sized according to available commercial sweater.

Yarn Handspun yarn of your choice for front bands and I-cord trim, in matching or contrasting colors to commercial sweater. The yarn used here was spun by Linda Ligon.

Needles 32" (80 cm) circular (cir) in size appropriate for your handspun yarn.

Notions Contrasting cotton embroidery thread; sharp-point sewing needle and thread to match commercial sweater; crochet hook in size appropriate for your handspun yarn; two double-pointed needles (dpn) or a hand-crank I-cord maker; buttons in size and number as desired; tapestry needle.

Front Bands

Measure across the sweater and find the exact center front. With contrasting embroidery thread and sewing needle, stitch a reference line along the center front, following a single column of sts to keep the line straight.

Fold the sweater along the center line. Join handspun to top right of the center line near the neckband, and work a line of slip-stitch crochet (see Glossary, page 122) parallel to and several stitches away from the center line as follows: Insert the crochet hook underneath an entire single stitch, hook a loop of handspun, and pull it through—1 loop on hook. *Insert the hook underneath the next stitch down in the same column (or more than one stitch

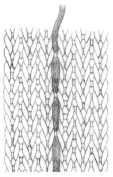

Stitch a reference line along the center front.

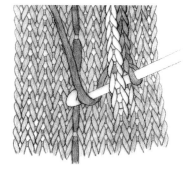

With handspun, work a row of slip-stitch crochet parallel to the marked center line.

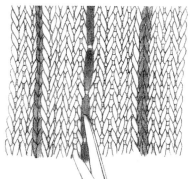

Cut the sweater open along the marked center line between the two lines of crochet stitches.

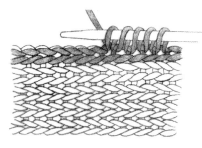

Pick up and knit stitches along the crocheted line of handspun.

Now, carefully cut along the marked center line, being careful not to cut through the handspun. As I like to say, you have "cardiganized" the sweater.

Using the circular needle and handspun yarn, pick up and knit stitches along the slip-stitch line of handspun at the left front for button band, adjusting the pick-up rate so that the knitted fabric doesn't pucker or gap.

Work the edging pattern of your choice (garter stitch is shown here) until the button band measures 1–2 inches (2.5–5 cm). Bind off all stitches. Mark positions for buttonholes on the right front of the garment, the lowest about 1" (2.5 cm) up from the lower edge, the highest 1" (2.5 cm) below the neck edge, and the rest of the buttonholes evenly spaced in between. Work buttonhole band as for button band for about 1/2–1 inch (1.3–2.5 cm). On the next row, work your choice of buttonhole method at each marked button position. Cont in garter st until buttonhole band measures 1–2 inches (2.5–5 cm) as for button band. Bind off all stitches.

Collar

With the same handspun or a different yarn to match the sweater, knit several yards of 3-stitch I-cord (see Glossary, page 123). Bind off all stitches. With sewing needle and matching thread, sew the I-cord around the neck opening in irregular loops as shown.

Finishing

With yarn threaded on tapestry needle, weave in ends. Block front bands lightly, if necessary. Sew buttons to button band opposite buttonholes.

down if your handspun is thick), hook another loop of handspun, and draw it through the loop already on the hook—1 loop remains on hook. Repeat from * until you have reached the lower edge, then fasten off the handspun. Turn sweater upside down, join handspun to lower left side of center line near the lower edge, and repeat for the other side of the marked center line, this time working from the lower edge to the neck so that both lines of slip-stitch crochet show on the right side of the knitting. Try to work the same number of slip stitches on each side.

Lynne Vogel

Lynne Vogel is the author of *The Twisted Sister Sock Workbook* (Interweave Press, 2002) and a prolific, award-winning knitter and spinner. She's worked as a needlepoint designer, painter, and fiber artist. Lynne lives in Sewanee, Tennessee, with her husband and dog, both of whom are also nature enthusiasts.

Lynne draws inspiration from her surroundings: this isn't difficult when you're living among the trees, reservoirs, and hills of southern Tennessee. During my visit, Lynne gave a slide-show presentation on how she uses nature to see colors that end up in her work. A fall landscape filled with leaves, summer flowers, and the thousands of shades of green each spring all make their way into her spinning and knitting in the surprising combinations found in nature. This from someone who initially resisted learning to spin! As Sandy Sitzman (see page 119) tells it, she encouraged (which may be too mild a word—the reality may be closer to "forced") Lynne to learn spinning several years ago because Sandy couldn't keep up with the handspun demand in Lynne's knitting designs.

Looking at the knitted garments Lynne designed for a gallery show at the Shakerag workshops in Tennessee, you would think she'd been spinning for decades instead of just a few years. Each piece showcased careful juxtapositions of color. The sweater shown here, a collaborative work by Lynne and West Coast fiber artist Lori Lawson, had dozens upon dozens of uniquely colored bits of handspun, each individually dyed, spun, and knitted into place. Like a Vermeer painting, the piece is a one-of-a-kind work of art. Textiles are arguably equal to fine art when such care is given to each component of the work.

Visit Lynne's website at www.handspuncentral.blogspot.com

Mind's Eye Hat

Shannon Okey

This hat is named after my friend Lucy Lee's yarn shop in Cambridge, Massachusetts. Lucy taught me to spin, and somewhere along the line, taught me the basic shaping for this hat. It remains my favorite hat to knit, year after year, because it is so infinitely variable depending on the yarns used. Next time you're in Porter Square, stop by and check out Lucy's hand-dyed wonders.

Hat

With cir needle, CO 74 (84) sts. Place marker (pm) and join for working in the rnd, being careful not to twist sts. Knit every rnd until piece measures 4½ (5)" (11.5 [12.5] cm) from CO. Knit 1 rnd, dec 4 sts evenly spaced—70 (80) sts rem. Dec for crown as foll, changing to dpn when there are too few sts to fit around cir.

Finished Size About 21 (24)" (53.5 [61] cm) head circumference and 7 (7½)" (18 [19] cm) tall with lower edge allowed to roll. Shown in size 24" (61 cm).

Yarn CYCA #5 Bulky (chunky-weight) yarn: about 100 yd (91 m). *Shown here:* Hand-dyed, handspun Corriedale wool yarn by Shannon Okey.

Needles Size 8 (5 mm): 16" (40 cm) circular (cir) and set of 4 double-pointed (dpn).

Notions Marker (m); tapestry needle.

Gauge About 14 sts and 26 rnds = 4" (10 cm) in St st worked in the rnd. Your handspun yarn and gauge may vary.

Dec Rnd 1: *K8, k2tog tbl (see Glossary, page 122); rep from *—63 (72) sts rem. Knit 1 rnd even.

Dec Rnd 2: *K7, k2tog tbl; rep from *—56 (64) sts rem. Knit 1 rnd even.

Dec Rnd 3: *K6, k2tog tbl; rep from *—49 (56) sts rem. Knit 1 rnd even.

Dec Rnd 4: *K5, k2tog tbl; rep from *—42 (48) sts rem. Knit 1 rnd even.

Dec Rnd 5: *K4, k2tog tbl; rep from *—35 (40) sts rem. Knit 1 rnd even.

Dec Rnd 6: *K3, k2tog tbl; rep from *—28 (32) sts rem. Knit 1 rnd even.

Dec Rnd 7: *K2, k2tog tbl; rep from *—21 (24) sts rem.

Dec Rnd 8: *K1, k2tog tbl; rep from *—14 (16) sts rem.

Dec Rnd 9: *K2tog tbl; rep from *—7 (8) sts rem. Cut yarn, leaving a 10" (25.5 cm) tail.

Finishing

Thread tail on tapestry needle, draw through rem sts, pull tight to close top, and fasten off on WS. Weave in loose ends.

Sandy Sitzman

Sandy Sitzman is a fiber enabler par excellence. Called the "Twisted Mom" by her circle of Twisted Sisters, she has introduced countless fiber artists (among them Lynne Vogel; see page 117) to spinning. Her business, Wool-gatherings, supplied spinners with beautiful hand-dyed fibers for many years. She lives in a geodesic dome nestled among vineyards and garden patches outside Portland, Oregon, with her husband and two playful dogs, both of whom have plenty of undercoat that would probably be spinnable. Although other fiber-bearing animals she once lived with are gone now, their spirits remain in yarn hanging from the loom in her upstairs balcony, aplaca batts in the studio, old hay in the barn, and a nicely fertilized compost heap.

Sandy is well-known for her multicolor rovings and batts, as well as the large Patrick Green drumcarder she once used to produce them. The "Crayons" roving she makes can be spun into a wondrous succession of colors, whether plain or plied against themselves. When she dyes, Sandy pours the colors directly onto the wet roving (she doesn't dab it on with a brush or other utensil), which gives an organic, random quality to the colors. The sweater Sandy's wearing in this photo, self-designed, hand-dyed, and handspun, is knitted from side to side, a method she recommends when using yarns that knit up at variable gauges.

Visit Sandy's website at www.woolgatherings.com

Glossary

Abbreviations

beg	begin(s); beginning	RS	right side
BO	bind off	sl	slip
CC	contrast color	sl st	slip st (slip pwise unless otherwise indicated)
cm	centimeter(s)		
cn	cable needle		
CO	cast on	ssk	slip 2 sts kwise, one at a time, from the left needle to right needle, insert left needle tip through both front loops and knit together from this position (1 st decrease)
dec(s)	decrease(s); decreasing		
dpn	double-pointed needles		
g	gram(s)		
inc(s)	increase(s); increasing		
k	knit		
k1f&b	knit into the front and back of same st	St st	stockinette stitch
kwise	knitwise, as if to knit	tbl	through back loop
m	marker(s)	tog	together
MC	main color	WS	wrong side
mm	millimeter(s)	wyb	with yarn in back
M1	make one (increase)	wyf	with yarn in front
p	purl	yd	yard(s)
p1f&b	purl into front and back of same st	yo	yarn over
		*	repeat starting point
patt(s)	pattern(s)	**	repeat all instructions between asterisks
psso	pass slipped st over		
pwise	purlwise, as if to purl	( )	alternate measurements and/or instructions
rem	remain(s); remaining		
rep	repeat(s)	[ ]	instructions are worked as a group a specified number of times.
rev St st	reverse stockinette stitch		
rnd(s)	round(s)		

Bind-Offs

Standard Bind-Off

Knit the first stitch, *knit the next stitch (2 stitches on right needle), insert left needle tip into first stitch on right needle (Figure 1) and lift this stitch up and over the second stitch (Figure 2) and off the needle (Figure 3). Repeat from * for the desired number of stitches.

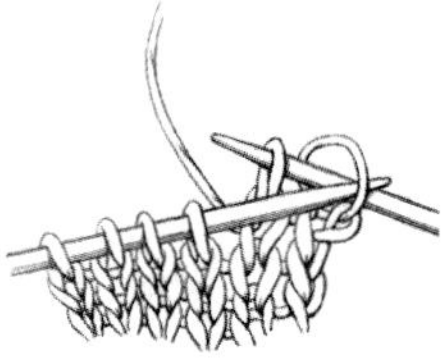

Figure 1

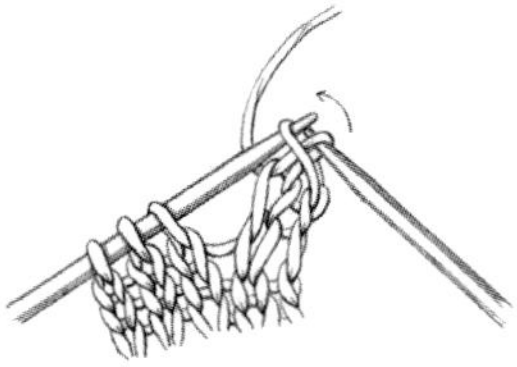

Figure 2 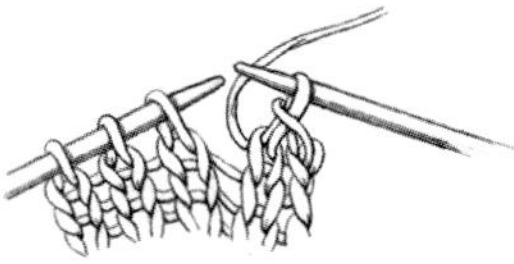   *Figure 3*

Three-Needle Bind-Off

Place the stitches to be joined onto two separate needles and hold the needles parallel so that the right sides of knitting face together. Insert a third needle into the first stitch on each of the two needles (Figure 1) and knit them together as 1 stitch (Figure 2), *knit the next

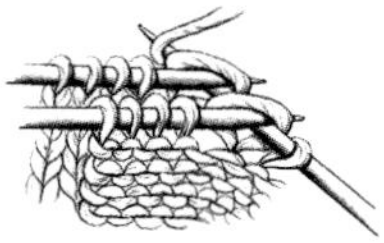

Figure 1

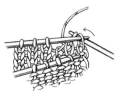

Figure 2   *Figure 3*

stitch on each needle the same way (2 stitches on right needle), then use the left needle tip to lift the first stitch on the right needle over the second and off the needle (Figure 3). Repeat from * until 1 stitch remains on third needle. Cut yarn and pull tail through last stitch to secure.

Cast-Ons

Backward Loop Cast-On

Leaving a short end, make a slipknot on the needle. *Tension

the yarn in your left hand and make a loop around your thumb, insert the needle in the loop, slip your thumb out, and gently pull the yarn to form a stitch on the needle. Repeat from * for the desired number of stitches.

Knitted Cast-On

Make a slipknot of working yarn and place on the left needle if there are no stitches already there. *Use the right needle to knit the first stitch (or slipknot) on left needle (Figure 1) and place new loop onto left needle to form a new stitch (Figure 2). Repeat from * for the desired number of stitches, always knitting into the last stitch made.

Figure 1   *Figure 2*

Long-Tail Cast-On

Leaving a long tail (about ½" to 1" [1.3 to 2.5 cm] for each stitch to be cast on), make a slipknot and place on right needle. Place thumb and index finger of your left hand between the yarn ends so that working yarn is around your index finger and tail end is around your thumb. Secure the yarn ends with your other fingers and hold your palm upwards, making a V of yarn (Figure 1). *Bring needle up through loop on thumb (Figure 2), catch first strand around index finger, and go back down through loop on thumb (Figure 3). Drop loop off thumb and, placing thumb back in V configuration, tighten resulting stitch on needle (Figure 4). Repeat from * for the desired number of stitches.

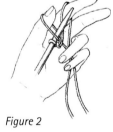

Figure 1   *Figure 2*

Figure 3   *Figure 4*

Provisional Cast-On

Make a loose slipknot of working yarn and place it on the right needle. Hold a length of waste yarn next to the slipknot and around your left thumb; hold working yarn over your left index finger. *Bring right needle forward under waste yarn, over working yarn, grab a loop of working yarn (Figure 1), then bring needle to the front over both yarns and grab a second loop (Figure 2). Repeat from * for the desired number of stitches. When you're ready to work in the opposite direction, place the exposed loops on a knitting needle as you pull out the waste yarn.

Figure 1   *Figure 2*

Crochet

Single Crochet (sc)

*Insert hook into the stitch or the second chain from the hook, yarn over hook and draw through a loop, yarn over hook (Figure 1), and draw it through both loops on hook (Figure 2). Repeat from * for the desired number of stitches. At the end of the row, chain 2 stitches and turn the work around. Begin the next row by inserting the hook into the second stitch from hook.

Figure 1   *Figure 2*

Slip-Stitch Crochet (sl st)

Insert hook into stitch, yarn over hook and draw loop through stitch and loop on hook.

Decreases

K2tog

Knit 2 stitches together as if they were a single stitch.

K2tog tbl

Knit 2 stitches together as if they were a single stitch, but insert the right needle through their back loops.

Ssk

Slip 2 stitches individually knitwise (Figure 1), insert left needle tip into the front of these 2 slipped stitches, and use the right needle to knit them together through their back loops (Figure 2).

Figure 1   *Figure 2*

P2tog
Purl 2 stitches together as if they were a single stitch.

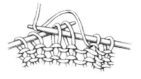

Slip 2 tog kwise, k1, p2sso (centered double decrease)
Slip 2 stitches together knitwise (Figure 1), knit the next stitch (Figure 2), then pass the slipped stitches over the knitted stitch (Figure 3).

Figure 1

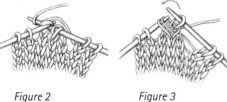

Figure 2   *Figure 3*

Slip 1, k2tog, psso
Slip 1 stitch knitwise, knit the next 2 stitches together (Figure 1), then use tip of left needle to lift slipped stitch up and over the knitted stitches (Figure 2).

Figure 1   *Figure 2*

I-Cord
Using 2 double-pointed needles, cast on the desired number of stitches (usually 3 to 4). *Without turning the needle, slide stitches to other end of needle, pull the yarn around the back, and knit the stitches as usual. Repeat from * for desired length.

Increases
K1f&b
Knit into a stitch but leave it on the left needle (Figure 1), then knit through the back loop of the same stitch (Figure 2) and slip the original stitch off the needle.

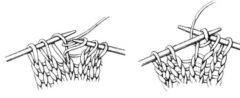

Figure 1   *Figure 2*

M1 (make one)
With left needle tip, lift the strand between last knitted stitch and first stitch on left needle from front to back (Figure 1), then knit the lifted loop through the back (Figure 2).

Figure 1   *Figure 2*

P1f&b

Purl into a stitch but leave it on the left needle (Figure 1), then purl through the back loop of the same stitch (Figure 2) and slip the original stitch off the needle.

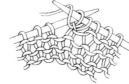

Figure 1   *Figure 2*

Yo (yarnover)

Wrap the working yarn around the needle from front to back, then bring yarn into position to work the next stitch (leave it in back if a knit stitch follows; bring it under the needle to the front if a purl stitch follows).

Pick Up and Knit

Work from right to left with right side facing. For horizontal (bind-off or cast-on) edges: Insert tip of needle into the center of the stitch below the bind-off or cast-on edge (Figure 1), wrap yarn around needle, and pull it through to make a stitch on the needle (Figure 2). Pick up one stitch for every stitch along the horizontal edge. For shaped edges: Insert needle between last and second-to-last stitches, warp yarn around needle, and pull it through to make a stitch on the needle (Figure 3). Pick up about three stitches for every four rows along the shaped edge. For heel gussets: Insert tip of needle into the front half of chain-selvedge stitch

(Figure 4) or into the entire chain-selvedge stitch (Figure 5), wrap yarn around needle, and pull it through. For a tighter join, pick up the stitches and knit them through the back loop (Figure 6).

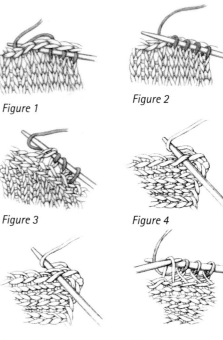

Figure 1   *Figure 2*

Figure 3   *Figure 4*

Figure 5   *Figure 6*

Seams

Backstitch Seam

Hold pieces to be seamed so that their right sides face each other and so that the edges to be

Figure 1   *Figure 2*

seamed are even with each other. Thread seaming yarn on a tapestry needle and join the pieces as follows: *Insert threaded needle through both layers from back to front, 2 stitches to the left (Figure 1), then from front to back 1 stitch to the right (Figure 2). Repeat from * for desired seam length, working right to left so that seaming yarn follows a circular path.

Kitchener Stitch

Place stitches to be joined onto two separate needles. Hold the needles parallel to each other, with the points facing to the right and so that wrong sides of the knitting face each other. With a threaded tapestry needle, work back and forth between the stitches on the two needles as follows:

Step 1: Bring threaded needle through first stitch on front needle as if to purl and leave that stitch on the needle.

Step 2: Bring threaded needle through first stitch on back needle as if to knit and leave that stitch on the needle.

Step 3: Bring threaded needle through first stitch on front needle (the same one used in Step 1) as if to knit and slip this stitch off the needle. Bring threaded needle through next stitch on front needle as if to purl and leave this stitch on the needle.

Step 4: Bring threaded needle through first stitch on back needle as if to purl (as illustrated), slip that stitch off, bring needle through next stitch on back needle as if to knit, and leave this stitch on the needle.

Repeat Steps 3 and 4 until all stitches have been worked.

Short-Rows

Work to turning point, slip next stitch purlwise to right needle, then bring the yarn to the front (Figure 1). Slip the same stitch back to the left needle (Figure 2), turn the work around and bring the yarn into position between the neeedles, for the next stitch, wrapping the slipped stitch with working yarn as you do so. When you come to a wrapped stitch on a subsequent row, hide the wrap by working it together with the wrapped stitch as follows: Insert right needle tip under the wrap (from the front if wrapped stitch is a knit stitch; from the back if wrapped stitch is a purl stitch), then into the stitch on the needle, and work the stitch and its wrap together as a single stitch.

Figure 1   *Figure 2*

Wraps per Inch (WPI)

The number of times a yarn can wrap around a ruler or pencil (or any other straight object) gives an estimate of the relative thickness of a yarn. Wrap your yarn around a ruler (without stretching the yarn) so that the wraps sit snug next to each other. Count the number of wraps in one inch. You may want to take the average of several measurements if your yarn is highly textured.

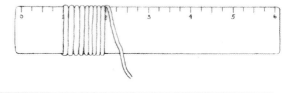

Yarn Weight

The Craft Yarn Council of America (CYCA) has devised a standard numbering system for reporting yarn weights. This system is used for the projects in this book.

STANDARD YARN WEIGHT SYSTEM						
Yarn Weight Symbol and Category Name	1 SUPER FINE	2 FINE	3 LIGHT	4 MEDIUM	5 BULKY	6 SUPER BULKY
Type of Yarns in Category	Sock, Fingering, Baby	Sport, Baby	DK, Light Worsted	Worsted, Afghan, Aran	Chunky, Craft, Rug	Bulky, Roving
*Knitted Gauge Range in Stockinette Stitch to 4" (10 cm)	27–32 sts	23–26 sts	21–24 sts	16–20 sts	12–15 sts	6–11 sts
Recommended Needle in Metric Size Range	2.25–3.25 mm	3.25–3.75 mm	3.75–4.5 mm	4.5–5.5 mm	5.5–8 mm	8 mm and larger
Recommended Needle in U.S. Size Range	1–3	3–5	5–7	7–9	9–11	11 and larger

*Guidelines Only: the above reflect the most commonly used gauges and needle for specific yarn categories

Resources

Commercial Yarns

Brown Sheep Company Inc.
100662 County Rd. 16
Mitchell, NE 69357
(800) 826-9136
www.brownsheep.com
—Lamb's Pride Worsted

Cascade Yarns
1224 Andover Park E.
Tukwila, WA 98188-3905
(800) 548-1048
www.cascadeyarns.com
—Eco Wool, Cascade 220

JCA Inc. (Reynolds)
35 Scales Ln.
Townsend, MA 01469
—Reynolds Lopi

Knitting Fever Inc. (Noro)
PO Box 336
315 Bayview Ave.
Amityville, NY 11701
(516) 546-3600
www.knittingfever.com
—Noro Silk Garden
—Noro Kureyon

Malabrigo Yarn
www.malabrigoyarn.com
sales@malabrigoyarn.com
—Malabrigo Merino

Norwegian Spirit Inc.
N27 W23713 Paul Rd., Unit G
Pewaukee, WI 53072
www.spirit-norway.com
—Lanet Superwash

Note: Many of the following spinners and farms are open by appointment only; please contact them before visiting.

Fibers and Handspun Yarns

Ashford Handicrafts Ltd.
415 West St.
PO Box 474
Ashburton, New Zealand
www.ashford.co.nz
Distributed in the U.S. by Foxglove
Fiberarts Supply
8040 NE Day Rd. West, Ste. 4F
Bainbridge Island, WA 98110
(206) 780-2747
www.foxglovefiber.com cindy@
foxglovefiber.com

Ashland Bay Trading Co.
PO Box 2613
Gig Harbor, WA 98335
www.ashlandbay.com

Baa Baa Yarn/Kirsten Hirsch
www.baabaayarn.com

Fleece Artist
www.fleeceartist.com
kathryn@fleeceartist.com

Hatchtown Farm
Pam and Jim Child
82 Sproul Hill Rd.
Bristol, ME 04539-3211
(207) 563-5851
www.hatchtownfarm.com
spindlegary@hatchtownfarm.com

Kristen Welsh
skalolazka2001@yahoo.com

Houndscroft Farm/Tamara Lepianka
www.houndscroftfarm.com info@
houndscroftfarm.com

Luxe/Natasha Fialkov
www.luxefibre.com
Natashaluxe@luxefibre.com

Morehouse Farm
2 Rock City Rd.
Red Hook, NY 12571
(845) 758-3710; (866) 470-4852
www.morehousefarm.com
CustomerService@
Morehousefarm.com

Pluckyfluff/Lexi Boeger
www.pluckyfluff.com
pluckyfluff@hotmail.com

Snapcrafty/Sandra Durkin
www.snapcrafty.com
sandra@snapcrafty.com

Sithean Fibers
www.sitheanfibers.com
sitheanj@dotnet.com

Winderwood Farm
Robert Smith
4934 State Rt. #245
Naples, NY 14512
(585) 374-8504; (877) 287-2501;
http://stores.ebay.com/WINDER-
WOOD-FARM

General Spinning Supplies

Nancy's Knit Knacks
104 Hobble Brook Ct.
Cary, NC 27511
(800) 731-5648
www.nancysknitknacks.com
—WPI gauges, portable lazy kates,
yarn meters

The Spinner's and Weaver's
Housecleaning Pages
www.together.net/~kbruce/
kbbspin.html
—Used spinning wheels and fiber
equipment

Spindles

Bonkers Handmade Originals
www.bonkersfiber.com
bonkers@bonkersfiber.com

Crowhill House Fiberworks
www.crowhillhouse.com

Hatchtown Farm
www.hatchtownfarm.com

Jonathan and Sheila Bosworth
www.journeywheel.com

Lynne Vogel
www.handspuncentral.blogspot.com

Schacht Spindle Co. Inc.
6101 Ben Pl.
Boulder, CO 80301
(303) 442-3212
www.schachtspindle.com
info@schachtspindle.com

Spindolyn
www.knittinganyway.com

Wheels

Ashford Handicrafts Ltd.
See listing under Fibers and
Handspun Yarns.

Kromski
Distributed in the U.S. by New
Voyager Trading
PO Box 468
Murfreesboro, NC 27855
(252) 398-4396
www.newvoyager.com/kromski.html

Journey Wheel
Jonathan and Sheila Bosworth
29 Main St.
Acton, MA 01720
(978) 264-0584
www.journeywheel.com
sheilabb@earthlink.net

Louët
Distributed in the U.S. by Louet Sales
808 Commerce Park Dr.
Ogdensburg, NY 13669
(613) 925-4502
info@louet.com

Majacraft Limited
Oropi Rd.
RD3 Tauranga, New Zealand
www.magacraft.co.nz
support@majacraft.co.nz

Schacht Spindle Co. Inc.
See listing under Spindles.

Web and Print Resources

Author Shannon Okey
www.knitgrrl.com
book website: www.spintoknit.com

KnittySpin
www.knittyspin.com
—The spinning-sister to Knitty.com

Department of Animal Science
Oklahoma State University
www.ansi.okstate.edu/breeds
—Information and photos of fiber
animal breeds

Index